Convergent Thinking for ADVANCED LEARNERS

Grades 3–5

Convergent Thinking for Advanced Learners, Grades 3–5 will teach students how to approach problems with a critical and evidence-based mindset.

Convergent thinking is a skill which helps students arrive at defensible solutions. Working through the lessons and handouts in this book, students will learn strategies and specific academic vocabulary in the sub-skills of observation, using evidence, considering perspectives, reflection, and deduction to find accurate solutions. This curriculum provides cohesive, scaffolded lessons to teach each targeted area of competency, followed by authentic application activities for students to then apply their newly developed skill set.

This book can be used as a stand-alone gifted curriculum or as part of an integrated curriculum. Each lesson ties in both reading and metacognitive skills, making it easy for teachers to incorporate into a variety of contexts.

Emily Hollett and **Anna Cassalia** are award-winning gifted educators and instructional differentiation coaches with Williamson County Schools, Tennessee.

Discover the other books in the Integrated Lessons in Higher Order Thinking Skills series

Available from Routledge
(www.routledge.com)

Analytical Thinking for Advanced Learners, Grades 3–5
Emily Hollett and Anna Cassalia

Divergent Thinking for Advanced Learners, Grades 3–5
Emily Hollett and Anna Cassalia

Evaluative Thinking for Advanced Learners, Grades 3–5
Emily Hollett and Anna Cassalia

Visual-Spatial Thinking for Advanced Learners, Grades 3–5
Emily Hollett and Anna Cassalia

Convergent Thinking for ADVANCED LEARNERS

Grades 3–5

Emily Hollett
and
Anna Cassalia

NEW YORK AND LONDON

Cover image: © Educlips

First published 2023
by Routledge
605 Third Avenue, New York, NY 10158

and by Routledge
4 Park Square, Milton Park, Abingdon, Oxon, OX14 4RN

Routledge is an imprint of the Taylor & Francis Group, an informa business

Library of Congress Cataloging-in-Publication Data
A catalog record for this title has been requested

ISBN: 978-1-032-21350-7 (hbk)
ISBN: 978-1-032-19925-2 (pbk)
ISBN: 978-1-003-26830-7 (ebk)

DOI: 10.4324/9781003268307

Typeset in Warnock Pro
by Deanta Global Publishing Services, Chennai, India

Access the Support Material: www.routledge.com/9781032199252

We would like to dedicate this book to all the students we've taught and will teach. You are the reason why we love this profession and wrote this series. We would also like to dedicate this series to our families, who have supported us unconditionally.

Contents

Acknowledgments

Special credit and acknowledgment must go to the many individuals whose work has paved the way for current educators like ourselves.

We draw great inspiration from the work of Sandra Kaplan, Alex Osborn, Sydney Parnes, Tamra Stambaugh, and Joyce VanTassel-Baska, whose curricular frameworks and research into best practice for teaching gifted learners are a driving force in shaping our own work.

Our guiding principles are grounded in National Association for Gifted Children (NAGC) programming standards, and we are so thankful for this organization's tireless dedication to gifted students, advocacy, and lifelong learning.

Clipart courtesy of Educlips. Used with permission under an extended license for hard copy books.

Handout font courtesy of Kimberly Geswein. Used with permission under a single font license.

Preface

The *Integrated Lessons in Higher Order Thinking Skills* series provides explicit instruction, targeted problems, and activities to teach gifted and high-ability students how to think using convergent, divergent, analytical, evaluative, and visual-spatial reasoning.

This unit was developed by and for teachers of gifted and advanced learners to provide explicit instruction in higher order thinking skills. In today's ever-changing, fast-paced world, our students require skill sets beyond rote memorization. Vast research supports the development of higher order thinking skills, including both creative and critical thinking skills which go beyond basic observation of facts and memorization. Systematically teaching these processes to students develops their ability to use these skills across the curriculum, building their ability to be "thinkers"—the ultimate goal of education.

The term "21st Century Thinking Skills" is widely used in education today, and while definitions vary, most educators agree: we need to be teaching our students not just *what* to think, but *how* to think. Learners in the 21st century must possess an array of thinking skills. They must be inquisitive about the world around them, and willing to ask questions and make mistakes. They must be logical and strategic thinkers. Logical thinking requires students to clarify problems while analyzing and making inferences based on the given information. Strategic, or deliberate, thinking requires students to think about where they are now in the learning process versus where they want to be in the future, and then determine action steps to achieve their goals.

Gifted and high-ability students require specialized instruction which is organized by key concepts and overarching themes. They need content which requires abstract thinking on a higher level than what is typically required by the general education curriculum. Beyond this, they require time to grapple with meaningful problems and derive defensible solutions. The *Integrated Lessons in Higher Order Thinking Skills* series provides scaffolded, focused lessons to teach these skills and give students authentic opportunities to develop these vital thinking processes.

Rationale

As Tony Wagner (Wagner and Compton, 2012) noted, our current educational system is obsolete and failing to educate our youth for the world of tomorrow. Wagner (Wagner and Compton, 2012) stated, "Students who only know how to perform well in today's educational system—get good grades and test scores and earn degrees—will no longer be those who are most likely to succeed. Thriving in the twenty-first century will require real competencies far more than academic credentials" (p. 20). Our educational system must help our youth discover their passions and purpose in life, and then develop the crucial skills necessary to think critically and creatively, communicate effectively, and problem-solve (Wagner and Compton, 2012).

Developing 21st-century thinkers requires a classroom environment that welcomes cognitive discourse and embraces the growth mindset approach. We must also teach our students that it is acceptable not to have an immediate answer; that some questions have many possible solutions, and indeed, some may never be answered; that persevering and being able to admit what you don't know is an important piece of learning.

Today's students must use metacognition, or awareness of and reflection on thinking processes. Metacognitive thinking is abstract in that one must analyze their thinking processes. Examples of this type of thinking might be asking oneself: "How did I get to that answer?" or "Where did my thinking go off track?" Learning to analyze the process of thinking is vital to problem-solving and learning. Teaching metacognitive strategies is a powerful way to improve students' self-efficacy, depth of thinking, and inquiry skills.

Students of the 21st century must develop problem-solving skills which require both creative and critical thinking. Creativity is a divergent thought process which involves generating new and unique possibilities. Critical thinking is a thought process which involves examining possibilities using a systematic, constructive method. Our students will be faced with unforeseen challenges that they must be able to think about creatively, critically, and strategically to solve. We, as educators, cannot possibly teach students everything there is to know, as the amount of new information available in the world is multiplying rapidly. Therefore, we must teach students to be inquisitive, analytical, innovative, evaluative, and curious. Learning and applying these thinking skills will prepare our students to solve the problems of tomorrow.

While we know the importance of higher order thinking, it is often left behind the "testable subjects" such as reading, writing, and arithmetic. This series was created to merge higher order thinking skills and the academic content students must grapple with in school. Systematic instruction in higher order thinking skills coupled with rigorous academic content is a relevant and engaging method to teach the students of the 21st century.

Higher order thinking consists of several distinctive and sophisticated thought processes. Central to these processes are the areas of systematic decision making (deductive reasoning), evaluative thinking, divergent (creative) thinking, concept attainment, and rule usage (analytical). In addition, visual-spatial reasoning has emerged as one of the most important skills for developing overall academic expertise, especially in technical fields. Each of these central processes is addressed in its own book within the *Integrated Lessons in Higher Order Thinking Skills* series.

Focus Strand: Convergent Thinking

Convergent thinking is the ability to determine a single, well-established, evidence-based answer. Convergent thinking skills help students approach problems with a critical and evidence-based mindset. Convergent thinking is a skill which helps students arrive at defensible solutions. It encompasses observation, logical reasoning, and inferencing. Working through the lessons in this book, students will learn strategies and specific academic vocabulary in the sub-skills of observation, using evidence, considering perspectives, reflection, and deduction to find accurate solutions. Developing convergent thinking skills helps students learn to be critical and thoughtful in their approaches to novel problems.

This book breaks down convergent thinking into five distinctive sub-skills: observing, using evidence, deduction, inferencing, and reflection. Each of these skills is taught explicitly through three lessons, increasing in complexity and abstraction, and culminating in an application lesson and activity. This approach allows students to build their convergent thinking skills incrementally and apply each skill as it develops. By completing all lessons in this book, students will be able to apply convergent thinking skills and strategies to a variety of problems, situations, and contexts.

Conceptual Framework

This curriculum is targeted for third through fifth grade gifted and high-ability students. Each of the five Thinking Skills units will provide students ways to develop problem-solving skills which require both creative and critical thinking. Frameworks for questioning and methodology were drawn from several research-based sources, including the Depth and Complexity Framework (Kaplan and Gould), the Paul-Elder Critical Thinking Framework, Visual Thinking Strategies (Harvard University's Project Zero).

Working through the lessons in this book, students will make connections by thinking in ways that incorporate elements of the Depth and Complexity Framework, such as thinking like a disciplinarian, connecting to universal themes, reasoning using question stems derived from the icons/elements, and examining problems through the lens of the content imperatives. Students will develop critical thinking skills based upon the elements of the Paul-Elder Critical Thinking Framework by applying thinking standards such as logic, precision, relevance, and depth to elements of problems such as inferences and assumptions in order to develop the intellectual traits of a critical thinker. Visual thinking routines are also incorporated to help scaffold students' metacognitive processes. Each of these research-based frameworks is embedded within the lessons in the form of question stems, instructional processes, graphic organizers, and methodology.

Each unit in the series uses explicit instruction to directly and systematically teach students how to think. Research shows that the most empirically supported method for teaching critical thinking is explicit instruction (Abrami, Bernard, Borokhovski, Wade, Surkes, Tamim, and Zhang, 2008). Using explicit instruction makes the learning outcomes clear.

Students are provided with clear, specific objectives. The unit lessons are broken down into manageable chunks of information. The teacher models the thinking skill with clear explanations and verbalizes their thinking process. Students are taught specific ways to reason and problem-solve. Students then practice the skills while the teacher provides feedback. At the conclusion of each lesson, students are asked to think metacognitively about their own learning.

Lesson Format and Guidelines

Each *Integrated Lessons in Higher Order Thinking Skills* unit follows the same format. Students are introduced to the higher order thinking skill through introductory lessons and materials to build schema in the targeted thinking area addressed in the unit. The introductory lesson in each unit provides a real-world connection. The overarching thinking skill is then broken down into five sub-skills. Each sub-skill is explicitly taught in three lessons. First, the students will be introduced to the sub-skill using an anchor chart. Then, students will participate in a warm-up activity teaching the sub-skill. Next, students will read and analyze trade books which highlight the sub-skill. Finally, students will participate in an activity learning to use the sub-skill. The third lesson in each sub-skill provides an opportunity for the students to apply the sub-skill in an authentic application activity. Key features of this unit as well as lesson summaries are outlined in Table P.1.

Unit Features

Materials

Included in this book are blackline masters of consumable materials to be used with students. Student handouts are provided with each lesson, and they include reading reflections, graphic organizers, full text stories for collaborative learning activities, formative "exit tickets," and others. Teacher materials, including anchor chart posters to provide visual cues for sub-skills, detailed lesson plans, and assessment rubrics, are also included. Other needed and optional materials are listed in lesson outlines. Links are provided for online resources, such as short video clips, and are accurate at the time of this book's printing.

Throughout the unit, trade books are used to teach and explore sub-skills in familiar contexts. These carefully selected trade books provide an exemplar for the lesson's focus. The recommended books are common and easily accessible; however, alternate texts are recommended to target each sub-skill (see Appendix B). Many of the texts may also have a digital version readily available as an online read aloud, accessible through a quick internet search.

In addition, some lessons utilize common classroom manipulatives such as attribute blocks, pattern blocks, or Tangrams. Printable versions of these manipulatives are also provided as handouts where they are used.

Teacher's note: It is always recommended that teachers preview any content (books, videos, images, etc.) before implementing it with students. Be sure to consider the context of the classroom and/or school in which the materials are to be used, being sensitive to the needs, experiences, and diversity of the students. Where possible, alternate trade books are suggested. Links provided are known to be accurate at the time of this book's publication.

TABLE P.1
Unit Overview

Introduction and Rationale Teacher introduction providing rationale for the unit.	❑ Outline of Thinking Skills: Teacher reference explaining an overview of each thinking skill and outcome. ❑ Standards Alignment: Unit alignment to both CCSS and NAGC standards are outlined.
Thinking Skill Overview This section provides introductory lessons and materials to build schema for students in the specific targeted thinking skill addressed in the unit.	❑ Frame of the Discipline: Think Like a Detective ■ Students gain understanding of authentic uses for convergent thinking skills within a career context. ❑ Artwork Intro: Students analyze a piece of classic visual art through the lens of convergent thinking to build thinking skill schema. ❑ Thinking Skills Avatar: Provides an ongoing touchstone for students to record key details and synthesize learning throughout the unit.
Sub-Skill 1: Observation In this section, students will develop the skill of using observation to look critically at the world around them.	❑ Lesson 1: Perspectives Matter ■ Students practice both crafting and understanding verbal descriptions of objects to better understand the power of perception. ❑ Lesson 2: Noticing Details ■ Students practice observing scenes to make predictions about events and items. ❑ Authentic Application Activity: Investigators and Eyewitnesses ■ Students personify various roles (investigators and eyewitnesses) to recreate scenes using as much detail as possible.
Sub-Skill 2: Using Evidence In this section, students learn methods for collecting and evaluating the validity of evidence to support claims/solutions.	❑ Lesson 1: Finding Evidence to Support Claims ■ Students practice citing evidence using familiar stories to make claims about characters. ❑ Lesson 2: Verifying Claims with Evidence ■ Students must evaluate evidence from a variety of sources in order to arrive at a solution. ❑ Authentic Application Activity: Validating Solutions with Evidence ■ Students will explore a mystery by gathering evidence from a series of clues, making a claim based on gathered evidence and possible solutions.

(Continued)

TABLE P.1
(Continued)

Sub-Skill 3: Inferencing In this section, students hone the skill of inferencing: using both observations and schema to make educated guesses about outcomes and ideas.	❑ Lesson 1: Using Observation to Infer ■ Students will observe a short wordless video to make inferences about characters' perspectives and changes over time. ❑ Lesson 2: Missing Information ■ Students analyze images to make inferences about missing text features. ❑ Authentic Application Activity: Shipwreck Scenario ■ Students apply their understanding of inferencing to a short fictional story, using inferences to extend the storyline to a satisfactory conclusion.
Sub-Skill 4: Deduction In this section students analyze clues to determine a single correct answer to a question or problem.	❑ Lesson 1: Using Clues to Confirm ■ Students use clues to confirm matches, inferences, and orders. ❑ Lesson 2: Using Clues to Eliminate ■ Students use clues to determine incorrect possibilities and arrive at correct solutions using process of elimination. ❑ Authentic Application Activity: Get a Clue! ■ Students will work with an extended logic puzzle to both confirm and eliminate their thinking, using logical reasoning to arrive at a solution.
Sub-Skill 5: Reflection Students will work through a variety of activities and models to understand how reflection plays a part in problem solving.	❑ Lesson 1: Reflecting on Experiences ■ Students complete challenging activities using multiple exposures to reflect on strategies, successes, and pitfalls. ❑ Lesson 2: Reflecting to Gain Perspectives ■ Students are given limited details over time to help them better understand that time builds perspectives and might change outcomes/solutions. ❑ Authentic Application Activity: Choose Your Path Story ■ Students must reflect on the impact of jumping to conclusions through reading and creating their own choose-your-path stories.
Appendix A	❑ Assessment Options
Appendix B	❑ Extension Options

Assessments

Possible *answer keys* and suggested *key understandings* are provided throughout the unit. These sample answers were created to help the teacher see the intended purpose for each lesson and illustrate the thinking skills students should be mastering. However, due to the open-ended nature of many of the lessons and activities, these answers should only be used as a guide and variations should be encouraged.

Blackline masters of assessment options are provided in Appendix A. Formative assessments are provided throughout the unit in the form of an exit ticket to conclude each sub-skill section. An overall unit rubric is provided along with diagnostic guidelines for observation. A whole-group checklist is provided for each sub-skill with diagnostic guidelines included. Teachers should review and select assessment options that best meet their goals for their students. It is recommended that students be assessed using a mastery mindset; growth in thinking skills is an ongoing process and all progress should be celebrated and acknowledged.

Time Allotment

Each lesson in this unit is intended to be taught in 60–90 minutes, but some lessons may take less or more time. In general, this unit can be taught in 15–20 hours of instructional time.

Unit Goals and Objectives

Concept

To develop conceptual awareness of convergent thinking skills using cross-curricular lessons, the students will:

- ❏ Develop an understanding of observation to look critically at the world around them
- ❏ Learn methods for collecting and evaluating the validity of evidence to support claims/solutions.
- ❏ Infer using both observations and schema to make educated guesses about outcomes and ideas.
- ❏ Use deductive reasoning to analyze clues to determine a single correct answer to a question or problem
- ❏ Reflect on data and processes to determine a single, well-established, evidence-based answer

Process

To develop deductive reasoning based on critical observation, valid evidence, and inferencing skills to determine a single correct answer, the students will:

- ❑ Gather information through observation, using the five senses
- ❑ Verify claims by finding facts and evidentiary supports
- ❑ Use prior knowledge to think about novel situations and problems
- ❑ Justify claims and inferences using evidence
- ❑ Use clues to deduce and confirm solutions
- ❑ Take time to reflect on facts
- ❑ Apply evidence to support explanations

Standards Alignment

Common Core State Standards (CCSS)

Standards are aligned with each of the five thinking skills targeted in the series, *Integrated Lessons in Higher Order Thinking Skills*. Specific thinking skills are noted using the following key (see also Table P.2):

- ❑ A: Analytical Thinking
- ❑ C: Convergent Thinking
- ❑ D: Divergent Thinking
- ❑ E: Evaluative Thinking
- ❑ V: Visual-Spatial Thinking

NAGC Programming Standards Alignment

Teaching thinking skills aligns with NAGC programming standards as best practice for gifted students:

- ❑ **Standard 1**: Students create awareness of and interest in their learning and cognitive growth
- ❑ **Standard 2**: Thinking skill aligned assessments provide evidence of learning progress
- ❑ **Standard 3**: Explicit instruction in thinking skills and metacognitive strategies is research-based best practice and meets the needs of gifted students for opportunities to develop depth, complexity, and abstraction in thinking and inquiry
- ❑ **Standard 5**: Competence in thinking skills promotes cognitive, social-emotional, and psychosocial development of students

TABLE P.2
CCSS Alignment

Language Standards	CCR Anchor Standards for Reading *1, 6, 7, 8*	❏ Draw logical inferences from text (C/E) ❏ Cite text evidence to support claims (C/E) ❏ Assess perspectives (A/C/D/E/V) ❏ Evaluate various content formats (A/C/D/E/V) ❏ Evaluate arguments based on evidence (E)
	CCR Anchor Standards for Writing *1, 3, 4, 8, 9, 10*	❏ Write arguments, citing text evidence and using valid reasoning (C/E) ❏ Write narratives (D) ❏ Develop written work appropriate to a variety of tasks (A/C/D/E/V) ❏ Evaluate and synthesize information from a variety of sources (E) ❏ Draw evidence to support analysis (A) ❏ Write routinely and for many purposes (A/C/D/E/V)
	CCR Anchor Standards for Speaking and Listening *1, 2, 3, 4*	❏ Collaborate for a variety of purposes with a variety of partners (A/C/D/E/V) ❏ Integrate information from a variety of sources (A/C/D/E/V) ❏ Critically evaluate speakers' perspectives (E) ❏ Present information, including evidence, in ways that allow others to follow lines of reasoning (A/C/E)
	CCR Anchor Standards for Language *3, 5, 6*	❏ Make effective use of appropriate language in a variety of contexts (A/C/D/E/V) ❏ Understand and make use of figurative language (A/D/E) ❏ Develop and apply academic vocabulary (A/C/D/E/V)
Mathematics Standards	CCSS for Mathematics: Practice Standards	❏ Make sense of problems and persevere in solving them ❏ Reason abstractly and quantitatively ❏ Construct viable arguments and critique the reasoning of others ❏ Model with mathematics ❏ Use appropriate tools strategically ❏ Attend to precision ❏ Look for and make use of structure ❏ Look for and express regularity in repeated reasoning *Applicable to problems presented in all Thinking Skills units.*

(*Continued*)

TABLE P.2
(Continued)

	CCSS for Mathematics: Operations and Algebraic Thinking *2.OA, 3.OA, 4.OA, 5.OA*	❑ Generate and analyze patterns and relationships (A/C/V) ❑ Represent problems both concretely and abstractly (A/C/V)
	CCSS for Mathematics: Measurement and Data *2.MD, 3.MD, 4.MD, 5.MD*	❑ Represent and interpret data (A/C/V)
	CCSS for Mathematics: Geometry *2.G, 3.G, 4.G, 5.G*	❑ Solve problems involving the coordinate plane (V) ❑ Solve problems involving lines, angles, and dimensions (V) ❑ Reason with shapes and their attributes (V)

Bibliography

Abrami, P.C., Bernard, R.M., Borokhovski, E., Wade, A., Surkes, M.A., Tamim, R., and Zhang, D. (2008). Instructional interventions affecting critical thinking skills and dispositions: A stage 1 meta-analysis. *Review of Educational Research, 78*(4), 1102–1134.

Common Core State Standards Initiative. (2022a) Common core state standards for English language arts & literacy in history/social studies, science, and technical subjects. http://www.corestandards.org/wp-content/uploads/ELA_Standards1.pdf.

Common Core State Standards Initiative. (2022b). Common core state standards for mathematics. http://www.corestandards.org/wp-content/uploads/Math_Standards1.pdf.

Dweck, C.S. (2006). *Mindset: The new psychology of success.* New York: Random House.

Kaplan, S. and Gould, B. (1995, 2003). *Depth & complexity icons, OERI, Javits project T.W.O. 2. Educator to educator. LVI.* J. Taylor Education, 2016.

NAGC Professional Standards Committee (2018–2019). 2019 Pre-K-grade 12 gifted programming standards. https://www.nagc.org/sites/default/files/standards/Intro%202019%20Programming%20Standards.pdf.

Paul, R, and Elder, L. (2020). *The miniature guide to critical thinking concepts and tools*. Santa Barbara, CA: Foundation for Critical Thinking.
Tishman, S., MacGillivray, D., and Palmer, P. (1999). Investigating the educational impact & potential of MoMA's visual thinking curriculum. http://www.pz.harvard.edu/projects/momas-visual-thinking-curriculum-project.
Wagner, T., and Compton, R.A. (2012). *Creating innovators: The making of young people who will change the world*. New York: Scribner.

Introduction to Convergent Thinking

Key Question: What is convergent thinking?

Materials

- ❏ Handout I.1a: Think Like a Disciplinarian: Convergent Thinking Like a Detective (one per student)
- ❏ Handout I.1b: Think Like a Disciplinarian: Convergent Thinking Like a Detective (one per student)
- ❏ Primary Source Artwork, projected to display for students to observe
  - Artwork: *The Arnolfini Portrait* by Jan Van Eyck, 1434
  - An online version of this artwork with zoom-in feature is available at https://www.nationalgallery.org.uk/paintings/jan-van-eyck-the-arnolfini-portrait.
- ❏ Handout I.2: Artwork Analysis (one per small group of students)
- ❏ Handout I.3: Convergent Thinking Avatar (one per student)

DOI: 10.4324/9781003268307-1

Introduction: Frame of the Discipline

- ❏ Tell students that in this unit, they will be learning how to think using *convergent* reasoning. *Convergent thinking* means thinking through problems in order to converge (or come together) on a single correct answer.
- ❏ Discuss the following with students: when is it is important to have one single correct answer to a problem? Many students will point out that math is a great example of this, and this provides a great avenue for discussing processes in math that relate to convergent thinking. Point out to students that in math problems, we use convergent thinking: we look for clues (numbers, information to help us solve), we reflect on our answers to make sure they are reasonable, and we use what we know to find what we don't know (inferencing). Bridge the discussion by reminding students that math problems are not the only type of problems that use convergent thinking—many situations call for this special type of thinking. In this unit, you will be learning more about how the convergent thinking process works using a variety of interesting problems that all require *one single correct answer.*
- ❏ Distribute Handout I.1a/I.1b. Read aloud with students the article "Convergent Thinking Like a Detective" (Handout I.1a).
- ❏ Work through the questions on Handout I.1b, Think Like a Disciplinarian: Convergent Thinking Like a Detective. Ensure that students are making connections between the thinking processes necessary for convergent thinking and how a real expert uses these processes (see Box I.1 for key understandings).

Box I.1: Framing the Thinking of a Detective Key Understandings

- ❏ *What questions do detectives ask?*
  - ■ Detectives ask questions such as *why, how, when, who,* and *what.*
  - ■ Detectives seek to gather as much information as possible about each problem.
- ❏ *What tools or thinking skills does a detective need?*
  - ■ Detectives need to make great observations, take notes, and organize their thinking.
  - ■ Detectives use thinking skills like reflection, seeking connections, and inferencing.

Handout I.1a: Think Like a Disciplinarian

Convergent Thinking Like a Detective

Name: ____

Detectives are people who work to solve crimes or mysteries. Sometimes, these are people who work for the police department and are detectives for their job. Other times, regular people can act as detectives, like when you try and find where your little brother hid your favorite pair of shoes. One thing all detectives have in common is their ability to think in certain ways. Detectives use **convergent thinking** skills to solve problems. This is a specific way of thinking that helps detectives come up with single solutions to problems. **Convergent thinking** means thinking through problems in order to converge (or come together) on a single correct answer. Using convergent thinking skills can work for anyone, and it's something everyone can practice!

The first step in convergent thinking is to **FIND AND ORGANIZE THE CLUES**. This means looking at a whole problem from many perspectives to see all the parts (**observation**), and then organizing the parts in a logical way to be able to think about them. Good detectives analyze clues, trying to make guesses based on what they know (**inferencing**). They work to be able to organize them in meaningful ways, using some clues to eliminate others and narrow down a solution (**deduction**). Sometimes, they tape all the clues up on a wall and then rearrange them based on their relationships to each other. Other times, they make an organized list of clues based on categories. The important part is to find each clue and think through how it can be organized.

The second step in convergent thinking is to **REFLECT ON ALL THE CLUES**. Sometimes after all the clues have been organized, there is not one clear answer. Taking time to think and reflect can help detectives see relationships and patterns they might have missed. This is also when a clue found later might be more meaningful to an earlier clue!

The third step in convergent thinking is to **PUT THE CLUES TOGETHER.** Once the clues are organized, and detectives have had some time to think, they are able to see the 'big picture'. Putting the clues together works just like a puzzle—each clue is its own separate piece, but together, they make one large solution: like a work of art!

The final step in convergent thinking is to **FIND AND REPORT THE SOLUTION**. Once all the clues are put together, detectives are able to arrive at the single solution that solves the mystery. Eureka!

Using convergent thinking can help you solve puzzles, mysteries, math problems, brain teasers, and more! Try and use these strategies as you read or think through any problem that requires a single solution. The more you develop your detective thinking using convergent thinking strategies, the better you'll get at it!

Handout I.1b: Think Like a Disciplinarian

Convergent Thinking Like a Detective

Name: ______________________________

What questions do detectives ask?

What tools or thinking skills does a detective need?

Describe the main purpose of a detective.

Why are detectives important in today's world?

How do detectives think about new information?

- ❑ *Why are detectives important in today's world?*
  - ■ Detectives seek to solve problems that might be tricky for other people. There will always be mysteries to solve.
- ❑ *How do detectives think about new information?*
  - ■ Detectives try to connect new information to what they already know, thinking about how various pieces of information work together to form a single solution.
- ❑ *Describe the main purpose of a detective.*
  - ■ Detectives seek to solve problems that have a single solution. These can be mysteries, puzzles, or other problems.

- ❑ Remind students that throughout this unit they will be thinking like a detective to solve problems and come to a single correct answer.

Primary Source: Artwork Analysis

- ❑ Prepare the artwork for display to students. In viewing the artwork, students will first view only a segment of the painting and will later be viewing the painting in its entirety. You will want to set up the students' view before revealing the first (partial) view to them—they will be using convergent thinking to consider how the segment relates to the larger, whole image. The image may be viewed through projection by visiting the online version of the painting at the UK National Gallery (link in materials list).
- ❑ Before displaying any portion of the image to students, prepare the image by using the National Gallery's online "zoom-in" tool. Narrow the viewable area by zooming in on the mirror in the upper center of the painting. (The mirror is on the back wall of the scene, just above where the two subjects' hands come together. It is round in shape with scalloping along the edges and a small, gold, tasseled string of beads hangs next to it on the wall.) The mirror should fill the view—you don't want students to be able to see very many other details. In the mirror, you should be able to see a reflection of two people standing together.
- ❑ Project *just the mirror portion of the painting* for students to consider. Discuss the image with students. Tell them that this is a portion of a painting by Jan Van Eyck, a German painter. The whole painting is titled *The Arnolfini Portrait*, and it was created in 1434.
- ❑ Direct students to look carefully at the painting and think about it like a detective. Invite them to use each of their senses, observe carefully, and think about what they may already know to ask some questions

about the painting. If needed, guide students with question stems such as the following:
  - What questions do you have?
  - What clues can you gather from this portion of the painting?
  - What perspectives are shown/missing?
  - Where could we get more information?
  - What can you tell about the subjects of the painting?
  - What else do you still wonder?
- ❑ Give students the Artwork Analysis page (Handout I.2). Guide students through answering the questions in the first two sections on the page, examining just the small mirror portion of the painting. Connect schema for students by reminding them that primary sources offer vital clues for a special kind of detective: historians!
- ❑ After some time in whole group discussion, zoom back out slowly so that students have the entirety of the painting visible to consider. Discuss the painting as a complete image, using questions such as the following:
  - How does having the whole picture change your perspective?
  - What are your feelings about the painting?
  - What conclusions can you draw?
- ❑ Help students complete the third section of Handout I.2. Guide their discussion—how did changing perspectives allow us to draw better conclusions? (See Box I.2 for expanded key understandings to target on Handout I.2.)

Box I.2: Primary Source: Artwork Analysis Key Understandings

Close-up section: We appear to be looking at a mirror. We can see the backs of some people who are standing together. The mirror is ornate, it appears that the people in the image may be close.

- ❑ *What information may still be missing?* We don't know what the people look like—we cannot see their faces. We also don't know anything about what surrounds the mirror. We can only see a small segment of the room. We don't know the context of the image—why was it painted, and for whom?
- ❑ *Viewing the complete image*: We can tell that these people are likely married. The room looks plain, yet the people are dressed

Handout I.2: Artwork Analysis

The Arnolfini Portrait, Jan Van Eyck, 1434

Name: ____________________

Look carefully at this portion of a painting by Jan Van Eyck, a Germain painter. The whole painting is entitled *Arnolfini Portrait*, and it was created in 1434. What do you notice?

Now think like a detective. What clues do you see? What might be missing? What do you still wonder? Where could we get more information? What can you tell from this section alone?

Now look at the complete painting. How does having the whole picture change your perspective? What are your feelings about the painting? What conclusions can you draw?

Describe the overall painting. What would be most important to point out to someone else? How do you know?

very well. This seems like a portrait that wealthy people might have commissioned—although the room looks humble, so we can't be sure.

- ❑ *Overall takeaways*: It would be important to point out the level of detail present in the image. It's interesting that the artist took the time to paint a mirror that is complete with the reflection in it. This painting often leaves viewers with more questions than answers, which makes it fun to discuss and make hypotheses about.

- ❑ Remind students they are using convergent thinking when analyzing this painting. They used their senses to observe, looked for clues that helped them make meaning of the image, inferred some ideas about the artwork that they did not know, and reflected on how the smaller part they viewed first related to the whole painting.
- ❑ Invite students to fill out the final section of Handout I.2 independently. Share responses if time allows.

Thinking Skills Avatar

- ❑ The final introductory lesson involves students creating their own Convergent Thinking Avatar. Today, students will decorate their Avatar. Distribute Handout I.3.
- ❑ Discuss with students the concept of an avatar. An avatar is a symbolic representation of a person that can be used as a stand-in. As you move through the convergent thinking sub-skills in this unit, this page will serve as a touch point for students to connect the skills together into one representation of convergent thinking.
- ❑ Explain that throughout this unit they will be introduced to five learning targets:
  - Observation
  - Using Evidence
  - Inferencing
  - Deduction
  - Reflection
- ❑ As students complete each target learning skill, they will pause and reflect on the key details of each sub-skill. This is a time for the students to synthesize their learning and record the key ideas for each learning target. At the conclusion of each sub-skill, students will return to this page and illustrate their original avatar using their newly learned skill.

Handout I.3: Convergent Thinking Avatar

Name: ______________________________

CREATE YOUR CONVERGENT THINKING AVATAR

MAKE OBSERVATIONS

USE EVIDENCE

MAKE INFERENCES

USE DEDUCTION

REFLECT ON IDEAS

- ❏ Allow students time to illustrate their avatar (the outline in the top left box) to represent a convergent thinking character/avatar of their choice. The other five boxes will remain empty for now, being filled in as students complete each sub-skill in the unit.

Bibliography

Van Eyck, J. (1434). *The Arnolfini portrait.* London, UK: The National Gallery. https://www.nationalgallery.org.uk/paintings/jan-van-eyck-the-arnolfini-portrait.

CHAPTER 1

Sub-Skill 1

Observation

TABLE 1.1
Observation Sub-Skill Overview

Thinking Skill Outline	
Focus Questions	❏ What can you notice? ❏ How do your senses help you gather information? ❏ How is observation subjective? Objective?
Lesson 1	*Perspectives Matter* ❏ **Trade Book Focus:** *They All Saw a Cat* by Brendan Wenzel ❏ **Practice Activity:** Do You See What I See? Students practice describing observations to a classmate who cannot see the object being described.
Lesson 2	*Noticing Details* ❏ **Trade Book Focus:** *Flotsam* by David Wiesner ❏ **Practice Activity:** What Can You Tell? Students practice observing scenes to make predictions about events being depicted.
Authentic Application Activity	*Investigators and Eyewitnesses* ❏ **Practice Activity:** Using a series of two unique Observation Scenes, students will observe a scene for a short time and then test their observation skills and memories to recreate those scenes verbally without the aid of the picture.

DOI: 10.4324/9781003268307-2

Observation Lesson 1: Perspectives Matter

Objective: Develop an understanding of the subjective nature of observation.

Materials

- ❏ Handout 1.1: Observation Anchor Chart (one enlarged copy for the class)
- ❏ *They All Saw a Cat* by Brendan Wenzel (teacher's copy)
- ❏ Handout 1.2: Read Aloud Reflection (one per student)
- ❏ Collection of small, assorted household objects (such as a whisk, hairbrush, fork, pencil, sponge, etc.), each placed in an opaque bag like a brown paper lunch sack (enough objects for one per student)
- ❏ Handout 1.3: Mystery Object Recording and Reflection Page (one per student)

Whole Group Introduction

- ❏ Tell students that we will be discussing the thinking skill of observation. Ask for volunteers to share anything they know about observation already.
- ❏ Share the Observation Anchor Chart (Handout 1.1). Tell students that observation means using our senses to gather information. Some students may be familiar with observation only as looking at things with their eyes; tell them that good deductive thinkers use all their senses to gather information.

Read Aloud Activity

- ❏ Share the cover of the book *They All Saw a Cat* with the students. Ask if any students have cats at home and, if you have time, allow them to share a little about their pets.
- ❏ Tell students that this story is about how many different characters observe the cat they see. Ask students to think like detectives to try and discover why the cat looks so different for each character.
- ❏ Read the story aloud, pausing at various points to offer some think-aloud modeling of observation. Use statements/questions such as:
  - ■ I wonder why this picture is in color/black and white?
  - ■ I wonder why we see/don't see the cat's face?
  - ■ This is interesting, that's not what I see when I look at a cat!

Handout 1.1: Observation Anchor Chart

OBSERVATION

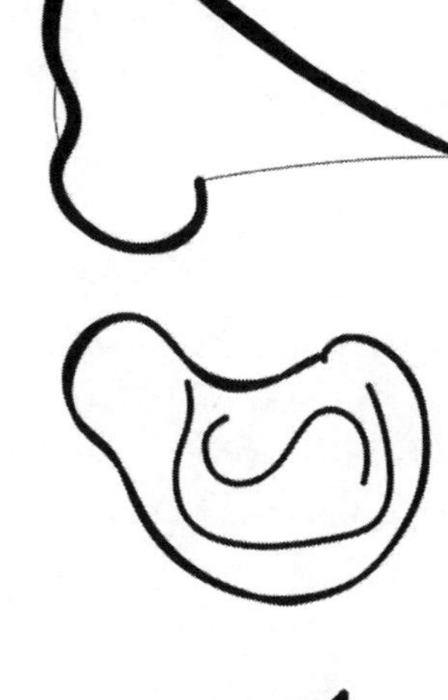

GATHERING INFORMATION
USING OUR SENSES

- ❏ After you finish the story, ask students to share what was most interesting for them. Which perspective was most surprising? Why? Make connections to the fact that the observation depends on the unique perspective of the one who is observing!
- ❏ Distribute the Read Aloud Reflection page (Handout 1.2). Direct students to carefully consider and answer the questions. When students have finished, discuss responses as a whole group (see Box 1.1 for expanded key understandings). Be sure to emphasize that observations in this case are very subjective, or varied, based on who is doing the observing.

Box 1.1: *They All Saw a Cat* Key Understandings

- ❏ *Book summary*: This book is mainly about how a cat is viewed from a variety of perspectives.
- ❏ *How the book shows observation*: Each person *observes* the cat in a unique way. Emphasize how the cat looks bigger, smaller, pixelated, or varied in color depending on who is viewing it.

Skill Development Activity

- ❏ Tell students that they will be participating in an activity in which their perspective as an observer will be tested. Model the activity once, with the teacher as the "observer" and the students as "listeners." Then, assign each student a partner to complete the activity twice more as a team.
- ❏ Distribute the Mystery Object Recording and Reflection Page (Handout 1.3) to each student.
- ❏ Steps for the activity:
  - ■ Prepare the activity by placing a variety of household objects into individual opaque bags (brown paper bags work well for this). Arrange the bags in a central location, like a front table or rug where they are accessible to students. You should have one bag available for each student. Divide students into pairs.
  - ■ The first partner will come to select one bag containing a "mystery object." Without the other partner being able to see that object, they will describe it based on their own observations of it. The object should stay inside the bag until the final reveal.

Handout 1.2: Read Aloud Reflection

They All Saw a Cat by Brenden Wenzel

Name: ____

Summarize the main idea of the story.	How did the book show **observation**?
How do YOU view a cat? Draw your view below, and then add a few adjectives to describe.	Which perspective was most interesting or surprising to you? Why?

Handout 1.3: Mystery Object Recording/Reflection

Name: ____

Listen carefully as a mystery object is described. Think about what you hear and try to determine what the object is. Draw the object exactly as it is described, and then make your best guess as to what it is.

MYSTERY OBJECT 1

Draw what you hear is observed.

What I think the object is...

What the object really is...

MYSTERY OBJECT 2

Draw what you hear is observed.

What I think the object is...

What the object really is...

REFLECTION: What was challenging about this activity? What was surprising? Was it easier to be the listener or the observer? Why? What could have made your observations more accurate/complete? Write a few sentences on the back to reflect on this activity.

  - The listening partner will draw what they hear their partner describing on the recording sheet. When they have finished their drawing, they will make a guess about what the mystery object is.
  - The mystery object will be revealed, and the listener will write down what it really was on their recording sheet.
  - The partners will then swap roles, with the partner who was the listener in the first round selecting their own "mystery object" from the array of bags; the original observer will have a chance to listen while the original listener observes.
- ❑ As a group, complete the reflection questions and then discuss the activity as a whole group.
- ❑ Guide students to gain a solid understanding that while personal perspectives have a strong influence on our observations, we can work to make our thinking more objective by being very descriptive and clear in our reports.

Observation Lesson 2: Noticing Details

Objective: Develop the skill of observation using all five senses.

Materials

- ❑ *Flotsam* by David Wiener (teacher's copy)
- ❑ Handout 1.4: Read Aloud Reflection (one per student)
- ❑ Figure 1.1: *A Sunday Afternoon on the Island of La Grande Jatte* by Georges Seurat, 1884 (either duplicated/enlarged or in a digital format projected so that all students can view)
  - Note: This painting may also be viewed online at https://www.metmuseum.org/art/collection/search/437658
- ❑ Handout 1.5: Artwork Observation Reflection Page (one per student or partnership)

Whole Group Introduction

- ❑ Remind students that in their last observation lesson, they discovered that observations can be subjective. Tell them that the goal of keen observation is to ensure that we gain as much information as we can. We do this with careful study and using each of our senses.
- ❑ Review the Observation Anchor Chart (Handout 1.1) with students.

Read Aloud Activity

- ❏ Read aloud from *Flotsam* by David Wiesner. As you read, pause to think aloud about how the perspective changes, and how the boy used each of his senses to notice and observe the beach area.
- ❏ Ask students probing questions, such as:
  - What senses were used to observe?
  - What did the boy notice? What did he miss?
  - If we were there, what other things could we observe with other senses, such as taste, touch, smell, and sound?
  - How did we gain a unique perspective?
  - How was the perspective limited? How was it expanded?
- ❏ Distribute the Read Aloud Reflection Page (Handout 1.4). Direct students to carefully consider and answer the questions. When students have finished, discuss responses as a whole group. See Box 1.2 for expanded key understandings. Be sure to emphasize that we must use each of our five senses to gain as much information as we can when observing.

Box 1.2: *Flotsam* Key Understandings

- ❏ *Story summary*: This story is wordless. Students will need to look carefully to find that it is mainly about how a lost camera has been used by a variety of "finders" to take photos from multiple perspectives. The perspective of each photo depends on time, place, and photographer.
- ❏ *How the story shows observation*: The boy uses observation to discover amazing images as well as how the camera has been found and passed along over time. He examines each photograph using several observational tools.
- ❏ *Sequence of story events*: The boy is searching for crabs on the beach when a wave crashes into him. Washed ashore, he finds the camera and has the film developed. He looks through the images, considers perspectives, and is amazed by the images. He then releases the camera back into the ocean to be found by another photographer in another location.
- ❏ *Cause and effect*: The boy discovers the camera by chance when a wave washes it ashore; as a result, his eyes are opened to the variety of life in the sea and the history of connection through the images across times.

Handout 1.4: Read Aloud Reflection

Flotsam by David Wiener

Name: ______________________________

Summarize the main idea of the story.

How did the book show observation?

Describe the sequence of events in the book.

What caused the boy to discover the camera?

What was the effect of the discovery on the boy?

What would have happened if the camera had been kept by someone who found it?

What does this book show about the importance of observation?

- ❑ *If the camera had been kept at any point*: If the camera had been kept by any of the photographers, the chain would have ended—there would have been far fewer images over time.
- ❑ *Importance of observation*: This book shows the importance of considering how our observations can connect with others and how each of our observations is unique.

Skill Development Activity

- ❑ For this activity, the students will complete an art observation reflection. Show them the painting *A Sunday Afternoon on the Island of La Grande Jatte* by Georges Seurat. Ask them to study the image and observe all its parts. Guide the students' observations with some clarifying questions based on facets of the painting, such as:
  - What season is it? How do you know?
  - Was this painting painted in modern times? Ancient times? How do you know?

Figure 1.1 *A Sunday Afternoon on the Island of La Grande Jatte*, Georges Seurat, 1886.

- What events are taking place here? Is there something exciting happening? How do you know?
- Are there any parts of the painting that strike you as strange or out of place? Why?

❑ Distribute Handout 1.5 to each student or partner group. Complete, independently or with a partner, the art observation reflection. Encourage students to record their thoughts as completely as possible, but also encourage them to discuss unanswered questions—what are we not able to determine based solely on the image? See Box 1.3 for expanded key understandings.

Box 1.3: Artwork Observation Key Understandings

❑ Students should notice several things about the artwork:
- It is likely set in a warmer month, on a warmer day. The people do not look to be particularly bundled up against the cold, and it looks sunny. Also, there are several people taking part in water sports (sailing, rowing) and others in sleeveless shirts, indicating a warm day.
- The artwork likely represents a weekend day or a vacation day; if it were a working day, there would likely be far fewer people.
- This is a painting of a time in the past—modern-day people have different ways of dressing and different leisure activities (i.e., there is no evidence of technology in this painting, but we do see girls making daisy chains, women doing needlework, etc.).
- Although many of the women hold umbrellas, it does not appear to be raining. Perhaps these were used more for shielding from the sun.
- It is likely later in the afternoon or early in the morning—the shadows on the ground are long, indicating that the sun is lower in the sky.
- Interestingly, there are several loose animals in this image (a dog, a monkey). We may wonder to whom they belong.

❑ Conduct a class reflective discussion about the following questions: How is observation powerful? How is it limiting?

Handout 1.5: Artwork Observation Reflection

Name: ______________________________

<table>
<tr><td colspan="2">Observe the painting carefully. Then, record your observations here. When you finish, discuss your observations with a friend. What did you observe that was similar? What did you observe that was different?</td></tr>
<tr><td>What is happening in the painting? Think about events, seasons/weather, activities, time period, etc.</td><td>What do you see?</td></tr>
<tr><td>What judgements can you make about the time and place where this was painted?</td><td>What connections can you make? (What does it remind you of?)</td></tr>
<tr><td>Pretend you were inside the world of the painting. What would you smell? Hear? Taste? Feel?</td><td>How does the painting make you feel? What emotions does it bring up? Why?</td></tr>
<tr><td>What do you like/dislike about the painting?</td><td>What do you wonder about the painting?</td></tr>
<tr><td colspan="2">Describe the painting to a friend who has never seen it before.</td></tr>
</table>

Observation Authentic Application Activity: Investigators and Eyewitnesses

Objective: Apply the skill of observation to an authentic context.

Materials

- ❏ Figure 1.2: Whole Class Observation Scene (one for the whole group, either projected or enlarged)
  - ■ Note: This image is available for viewing online at https://www.loc.gov/pictures/item/2017762372/
- ❏ Figures 1.3 and 1.4: Observation Scenes 1 and 2 (one of each for the whole group, either projected or enlarged)
- ❏ Handout 1.6: Check Your Memory! Questionnaire (one half-page per student)
- ❏ Handout 1.7: Investigative Journal (one per student)

Whole Group Introduction

- ❏ Review with students the necessary skills for observation. Share again the Observation Anchor Chart. Remind students that they should be on the lookout for interesting or noteworthy details but should also be paying attention to basic information as they observe a new scene.
- ❏ Tell the students that today they will be thinking like detectives to test their own observation skills. Preface the activity, saying something like, "In just a moment, I am going to show you a picture for 30 seconds. I want you to take that time to do your very best observation. Try to remember as many details as you can. After the time is over, I will hide the picture and we will answer some questions about it to test our observation skills."
- ❏ Pass out Handout 1.6, the Check Your Memory! Questionnaire (half page), to each student. They should keep this face down on their desk until after the picture has been shown—no peeking!
- ❏ Show the Whole Group Observation Scene (Figure 1.2) for 30 seconds (it is recommended that you share this in a large format, such as a poster or via projector using a document camera.)
- ❏ Hide the scene (Figure 1.2). At this time, students will turn their questionnaire pages over and will have 2–3 minutes to answer the questions to the best of their ability. Tell them that if they can't remember an

Handout 1.6: Check Your Memory!

Name: ______________________

Date: ______________________

Describe the scene. Give a 'big picture' of what it was about.

Who was involved? What details do you remember about the people?

Was there anything unusual in the picture that stood out to you?

Did you notice any time/date features?

What other details do you remember about the scene?

Name: ______________________

Date: ______________________

Describe the scene. Give a 'big picture' of what it was about.

Who was involved? What details do you remember about the people?

Was there anything unusual in the picture that stood out to you?

Did you notice any time/date features?

What other details do you remember about the scene?

Handout 1.7: Investigative Journal

Name: ____________________

Your job as an investigator will be to recreate the scene as accurately as possible. Interview as many eyewitnesses as you can to get an accurate idea of what happened in the scene. Take careful notes that you can refer to as you recreate the scene after your interviews. You can ask for any details you like but think through questions like the ones listed here. Good luck!

- **Where was the scene taking place?**
- **Was there anything unusual you noticed?**
- **Who was involved? Genders? Ages?**
- **What time of day was it?**
- **What were the subjects in the scene wearing?**

Witness: Details:	Witness: Details:
Witness: Details:	Witness: Details:
Witness: Details:	Witness: Details:

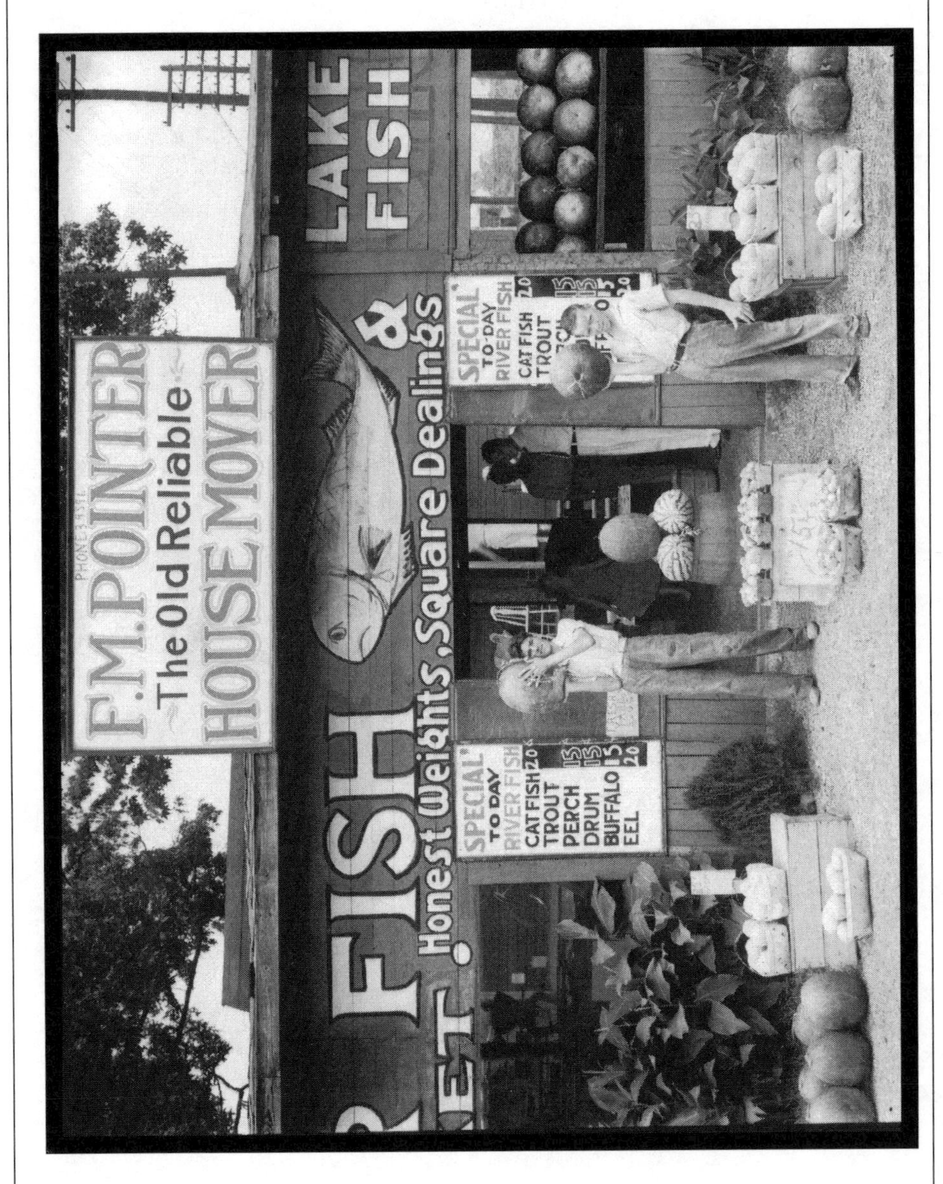

Figure 1.2 *Roadside Stand Near Birmingham, Alabama*, Walker Evans, 1936.

Figure 1.3 Observation Scene A (Bank).

answer, then they should give their best guess, but not spend too much time on any one question.

- ❑ At the end of the 2–3 minutes, have all students put their pencils down. Go through the questions together as a whole group, discussing where students agree/disagree on the answers to the questions.
- ❑ Show the Whole Group Observation Scene (Figure 1.2) again. Ask students what they got right, and what they remembered incorrectly. Discuss this activity, using questions such as:
  - What was challenging? Surprising?
  - What made things easier to remember?
  - What stood out?
  - Why do you think people remembered various parts of the scene in different ways?
  - How will this affect the accuracy of our observations?

Skill Development Activity

- ❑ Tell the students that they will now be able to apply their observation skills to play a fun game. Explain the concepts of investigators and eyewitnesses to the students, using the following definitions as needed.
  - Investigators are trying to gather information about something that they did not see with their own eyes. They use good questions to gather information from someone who has seen an event or image firsthand.
  - Eyewitnesses are those who have seen an event or image themselves. They have firsthand knowledge, as they were observers of the scene.
- ❑ Divide the class into two even sections: investigators and eyewitnesses. Be sure that all students know which role they will play. Assure students that in the next round, they will get to switch roles, so that each student has an opportunity to be both an investigator and an eyewitness.
- ❑ Show Observation Scene #1 (Figure 1.3) to *only* the eyewitnesses. (You may be able to send the investigators out of the room or have them turn around or put their heads down on desks to accomplish this.) Allow the eyewitnesses to study the scene for at least 1 minute, but no more than 2 minutes. Hide the scene.
- ❑ Invite the investigators to rejoin the whole group. Then, give them time to circulate the room, interviewing eyewitnesses. Encourage them to talk to as many eyewitnesses as possible to get the clearest possible picture of what happened in the scene. Allow 5–10 minutes for investigators to conduct interviews. Investigators might ask any question

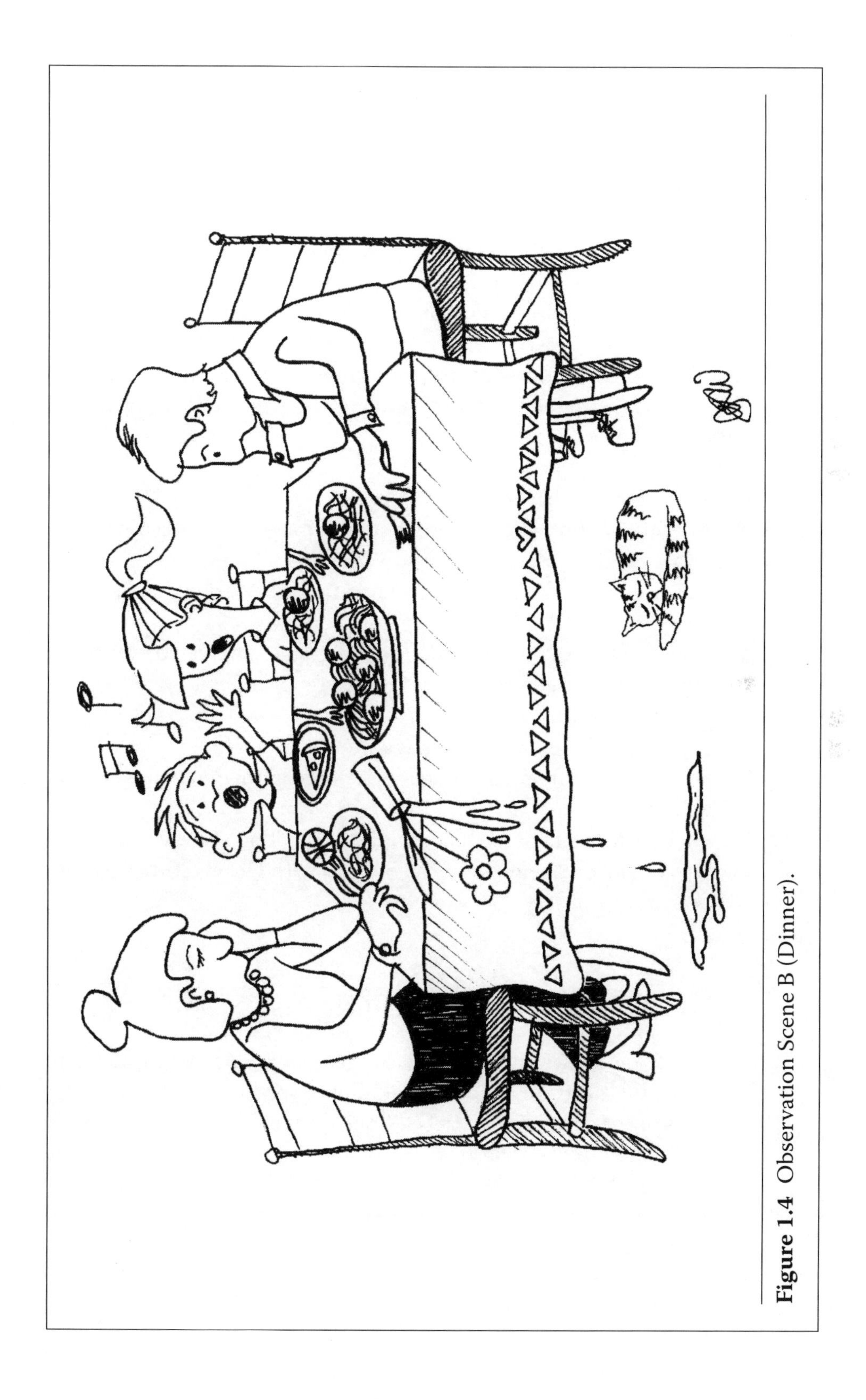

Figure 1.4 Observation Scene B (Dinner).

they wish in order to accurately reconstruct the scene. Some examples of questions might be:
- Where was the scene taking place?
- Was there anything unusual you noticed?
- Who was involved? Genders? Ages?
- What time of day was it?
- What were the subjects in the scene wearing?

- ❏ Stop the interviews and guide students to return to their seats. Elicit responses from investigators about the scene, keeping a list of details on the board for all to read. Remind the eyewitnesses that they shouldn't add ideas here; the investigators are trying to fill in as many details as they are able based only on their interviews. Ask the investigators to tell you about:
  - The setting of the scene
  - The characters in the scene
  - Anything noteworthy or strange/out of place for the scene
  - Other details they can recall or were told
- ❏ Discuss the results. Think about elements of the activity such as the following:
  - How much of the scene could the investigators reconstruct? Why?
  - Did any investigators get conflicting reports from eyewitnesses? What/why/how?
  - How many details were investigators able to include?
  - Did any eyewitnesses have strategies to help them remember what was in the scene?
- ❏ View the scene again as a whole group to reflect on accuracy.
- ❏ Swap roles and complete the activity again with Observation Scene #2 (Figure 1.4).

Observation Concluding Activities

- ❏ Distribute the Observation Exit Ticket (Appendix A). Ask students to reflect on their learning about the skill of observation. Allow time for students to complete the exit ticket. Use this as a formative assessment, to gain a better understanding of your students' readiness to effectively practice the skill of observation.
- ❏ If desired, complete the Group Observation Rubric (Appendix A) to track students' progress with the skill.
- ❏ If desired, use the Convergent Thinking Student Observation Rubric (Appendix A) to assess and quantify individual students' mastery.

- ❏ Ask students to retrieve their Convergent Thinking Avatar (Handout 1.3). In the Observation box, they should either record the main ideas about the thinking skill or illustrate their avatar using the skill of observation.

Bibliography

Roadside Stand Near Birmingham, Alabama; photograph by Walker Evans for the US Farm Security Administration/Office of War Information Black-and-White (1936).

A Sunday Afternoon on the Island of La Grande Jatte, by Georges Seurat. (1884). CC0/public domain.

Weisner, D. (2006). *Flotsam.* New York: Clarion Books.

Wenzel, B. (2016). *They all saw a cat.* San Francisco, CA: Chronicle Books.

CHAPTER 2

Sub-Skill 2

Using Evidence

TABLE 2.1
Using Evidence Sub-Skill Overview

Thinking Skill Outline	
Focus Questions	❏ How can we back up our claims, solutions, and arguments? ❏ How can we verify solutions with evidence?
Lesson 1	*Finding Evidence to Support Claims* ❏ **Trade Book Focus:** *Mother Bruce* by Ryan T. Higgins ❏ **Practice Activity:** Character Sketches—Students will support given claims that characters possess a variety of traits by finding evidence within a familiar story.
Lesson 2	*Verifying Claims with Evidence* ❏ **Trade Book Focus:** *The Stranger* by Chris Van Allsburg ❏ **Practice Activity:** Students will work with extended metaphor poems to make claims, and then will practice writing their own poems using evidence for a peer to make a claim about.
Authentic Application Activity	*Validating Solutions with Evidence* ❏ **Trade Book Focus:** *Seven Blind Mice* by Ed Young ❏ **Practice Activity:** Students will gather information from a variety of clues and informational texts, citing evidence to validate their conclusion.

DOI: 10.4324/9781003268307-3

Using Evidence Lesson 1: Finding Evidence to Support Claims

Objective: Develop the skill of finding evidence in familiar stories by explicitly citing details.

Materials

- ❑ *Mother Bruce* by Ryan T. Higgins (teacher's copy)
- ❑ Handout 2.2: Read Aloud Reflection (one per student)
- ❑ Handout 2.3: "The Tale of Peter Rabbit" story with annotation panels (one per student)
- ❑ Handout 2.4: Socratic Seminar Preparation Guide (one per student)
- ❑ Optional: Socratic Seminar Self-Reflection (Appendix A)
- ❑ Optional: Socratic Seminar Assessment Rubric (Appendix A)
- ❑ Optional: dice

Whole Group Introduction

- ❑ Introduce the skill of using evidence. Tell students that this convergent thinking skill requires them to find information that will support their solutions. Remind students that facts and opinions are different, and that evidence must be based upon facts in order to be defensible.
- ❑ Show students the Using Evidence Anchor Chart (Handout 2.1). Describe the icon in the center as being representative of how evidence from many sources comes together to formulate a single correct solution.
- ❑ Play "I'm thinking of a..." with the students. See if they can put your clues together to guess what you're thinking of. Start with a familiar item or object and reveal hints one at a time. Ask students to observe the room around them and see if they can guess what you're referring to by observing evidence about classroom objects. See Table 2.2 for some ideas, but try to use an object that the students can see within the classroom. Some hints are given, but you may also think of many others!
- ❑ Ask students: What evidence did you use to make your guesses? What other clues could we have used?

Handout 2.1: Using Evidence Anchor Chart

USING EVIDENCE

!

VERIFYING CLAIMS BY FINDING FACTS

TABLE 2.2
"I'm Thinking of a..." Starters

Chair	Trash Can
❑ It's something we use every day. ❑ It's [insert color]. ❑ It's hard, not soft. ❑ It doesn't move by itself. ❑ We each have our own. ❑ If we didn't have them, we would be very tired by the end of the day.	❑ This is something we use every day. ❑ It's [insert color]. ❑ It can get full. ❑ It can get messy. ❑ It can hold things. ❑ If we didn't have one, we would be in a mess. ❑ We must empty it.
Rug	**Jacket**
❑ It's soft. ❑ It's [insert color]. ❑ It lies around all day. ❑ It covers something. ❑ It's useful for decorating. ❑ It is not a necessary part of a classroom, but it is nice to have. ❑ You can sit or stand on it.	❑ This is something you wear. ❑ It comes in many colors. ❑ We usually wear them only in certain seasons. ❑ When we are inside, we usually take these off. ❑ They keep us warm in winter. ❑ If you didn't have one, you might get cold at recess.

Read Aloud Activity

- ❑ Read aloud from *Mother Bruce* by Ryan T. Higgins. At the beginning of the story, Bruce is described as "grumpy." The author gives several pieces of reasoning to describe how and why Bruce is "grumpy." Model thinking aloud, citing evidence from the text as you read this portion of the story.
- ❑ Pause as soon as you've discussed reasons why Bruce is grumpy. Ensure that students understand how the evidence points to this conclusion.
- ❑ Ask students to listen as you continue reading for other character traits that may also describe Bruce. If needed, display some sample character traits (Box 2.1) so that students have some ideas of potential describing words. Remind them that they should try and find evidence (things Bruce *says*, *does*, *thinks*, or *wants*) to support their ideas.

Box 2.1: Sample Character Traits

hard-working, intelligent, imaginative, curious, adventurous, stubborn, organized, unfriendly, timid, helpful, tender-hearted, thoughtful, friendly, shy, creative, thoughtful, honest, energetic, generous, active, brave, responsible, outgoing, honest, caring, controlling

- ❑ After reading, distribute the Read Aloud Reflection page (Handout 2.2). Ask students to recall the evidence pointing to the fact that Bruce is grumpy at the top. At the bottom, ask them to describe and support three additional character traits describing Bruce. See Box 2.2 for key understandings for the Read Aloud Reflection. Discuss as a group, refining students' thinking as needed.

Box 2.2: *Mother Bruce* Key Understandings

- ❑ *Story summary*: Bruce is a bear who lives alone and is described as "grumpy." When a flock of geese move in with him, he finds ways to be flexible in taking care of them.
- ❑ *Evidence that Bruce is grumpy*: He does not like sun, rain, or cute animals. His body language and facial expressions signal grumpiness.
- ❑ *Other character traits*: Bruce can be described using many traits. He is responsible in that he does take care of the geese. He is caring; he will not leave the geese to their own devices. He is hard-working; he cooks, cleans, and organizes his life around the geese. Students will be able to draw their own conclusions about traits that describe Bruce. Look for students to cite examples from the story to support their thinking.

Skill Development Activity

- ❑ Now, students will work with a classic story to support various claims. To randomly assign characters and traits, either have each student roll a die or number the students off, using 1–6. Assign characters and traits based on the following:

Handout 2.2: Read Aloud Reflection

Mother Bruce by Ryan T. Higgins

Name: ____________________

In the beginning of the story, Bruce is described as "grumpy". What evidence does the author give to support this?

Choose three other character traits that could be used to describe Bruce. Then, give evidence (proof) from the story to support your thinking. Remember, evidence is something that anyone could see, and could be based on things that Bruce SAYS, DOES, THINKS, or WANTS.

Bruce is…

I know because he…

Bruce is…

I know because he…

Bruce is…

I know because he…

    - First Roll/Number Assignment (character): *even* numbers will focus on Peter, *odd* numbers will focus on Mr. McGregor.
    - Second Roll/Number Assignment (trait): 1—clever; 2—thoughtful; 3—careful; 4—responsible; 5—stubborn; 6—tricky
- ❑ Distribute "The Tale of Peter Rabbit" (Handout 2.3) to students. They will record their character and focus trait at the top. As they read, they will find evidence to support their assigned trait and character. They may choose to either prove or disprove their assigned trait. Remind students to focus on things that their character *says, does, thinks,* or *wants.* Students should take notes on evidence supporting their given claim in the note-taking space on the right-hand side of each page of the story. See Table 2.3 for examples of evidence for each character and trait.
- ❑ As students work through their stories, scaffold support as needed. Scaffolds offered might include:
    - Circulating, encouraging, and reminding students to take notes and highlight/annotate their text. Students will benefit greatly from having these notes as they move into the Socratic Seminar.
    - Allowing students to work independently (above level), with a peer who has the same character and trait (on-level), or with more hands-on teacher support (below level).
    - Extending thinking by encouraging fast finishers to go back through the story to spot places where others might be able to cite evidence refuting their given claim. Ask them to come up with a counter-point argument in support of their given claim.
- ❑ When students finish, break the whole group into two segments: those who focused on Peter and those who focused on Mr. McGregor. Using a fishbowl method, (one group discussing while the other observes and then trading places), engage each group in a Socratic Seminar based upon the question: "What kind of person/character is ____?"

Socratic Seminar

- ❑ Socratic Seminar is a teaching strategy that provides students the opportunity to discuss a topic or concept to gain a deeper understanding. Socrates believed students learn best when provided the opportunity to come to an understanding themselves through thoughtful questioning. Socrates did not provide answers to his students' questions; rather, he responded to questions with more questions. This allowed the students to examine their own thinking and come to their own conclusions.

Handout 2.3: Finding Text Evidence

The Tale of Peter Rabbit by Beatrix Potter

Name: ______________________________

ONCE upon a time there were four little rabbits, and their names were—

Flopsy,

Mopsy,

Cotton-tail,

and Peter.

They lived with their mother in a sand-bank, underneath the root of a very big fir tree.

"Now, my dears," said old Mrs. Rabbit one morning, "you may go into the fields or down the lane, but don't go into Mr. McGregor's garden: your father had an accident there; he was put in a pie by Mrs. McGregor."

"Now run along, and don't get into mischief. I am going out."

Then old Mrs. Rabbit took a basket and her umbrella, to the baker's. She bought a loaf of brown bread and five currant buns.

Flopsy, Mopsy, and Cottontail, who were good little bunnies, went down the lane to gather blackberries; but Peter, who was very naughty, ran straight away to Mr. McGregor's garden and squeezed under the gate!

First, he ate some lettuces and some French beans; and then he ate some radishes; and then, feeling rather sick, he went to look for some parsley.

Character:

Trait:

Record EVIDENCE to help you prove your claim.

Handout 2.3: Finding Text Evidence

The Tale of Peter Rabbit by Beatrix Potter

Name: ____________________

But round the end of a cucumber frame, whom should he meet but Mr. McGregor! Mr. McGregor was on his hands and knees planting out young cabbages, but he jumped up and ran after Peter, waving a rake and calling out, "Stop thief!"

Peter was most dreadfully frightened; he rushed all over the garden, for he had forgotten the way back to the gate.

He lost one of his shoes among the cabbages, and the other shoe amongst the potatoes.

After losing them, he ran on four legs and went faster, so that I think he might have got away altogether if he had not unfortunately run into a gooseberry net and got caught by the large buttons on his jacket. It was a blue jacket with brass buttons, quite new.

Peter gave himself up for lost and shed big tears; but his sobs were overheard by some friendly sparrows, who flew to him in great excitement, and implored him to exert himself.

Mr. McGregor came up with a sieve, which he intended to pop upon the top of Peter; but Peter wriggled out just in time, leaving his jacket behind him.

And rushed into the toolshed and jumped into a can. It would have been a beautiful thing to hide in, if it had not had so much water in it.

Mr. McGregor was quite sure that Peter was somewhere in the toolshed, perhaps hidden underneath a flower-pot. He began to turn them over carefully, looking under each.

Character:

Trait:

Record EVIDENCE to help you prove your claim.

Handout 2.3: Finding Text Evidence

The Tale of Peter Rabbit by Beatrix Potter

Name: ________________________________

Presently Peter sneezed—"Kertyschoo!" Mr. McGregor was after him in no time, and tried to put his foot upon Peter, who jumped out of a window, upsetting three plants. The window was too small for Mr. McGregor, and he was tired of running after Peter. He went back to his work.

Peter sat down to rest; he was out of breath and trembling with fright, and he had not the least idea which way to go. Also he was very damp with sitting in that can.

After a time he began to wander about, going lippity—lippity—not very fast, and looking all around.

He found a door in a wall; but it was locked, and there was no room for a fat little rabbit to squeeze underneath.

An old mouse was running in and out over the stone door-step, carrying peas and beans to her family in the wood. Peter asked her the way to the gate, but she had such a large pea in her mouth that she could not answer. She shook her head at him. Peter began to cry again.

Then he tried to find his way straight across the garden, but he became more and more puzzled. There surely never was such a garden for cabbages! Hundreds and hundreds of them; and Peter was not tall enough to see over them and felt too sick to eat them. It was just like a very bad dream!

Character:

Trait:

Record EVIDENCE to help you prove your claim.

Handout 2.3: Finding Text Evidence

The Tale of Peter Rabbit by Beatrix Potter

Name: ______________________________

In the middle of the garden he came to a pond where Mr. McGregor filled his water-cans. A white cat was staring at some gold-fish; she sat very, very still, but now and then the tip of her tail twitched as if it were alive. Peter thought it best to go away without speaking to her; he had heard about cats from his cousin, little Benjamin Bunny.

He went towards the tool-shed again, but suddenly there was a most peculiar noise—scr-r-ritch, scratch, scratch, scritch. Peter scuttered underneath the bushes. Then some one began to sing 'Three blind mice, three blind mice!' It sounded disagreeable to Peter; it made him feel as though his own tail were going to be cut off: his fur stood on end.

After a time, as nothing happened, Peter came out, and climbed upon a wheel-barrow, and peeped over. The first thing he saw was Mr. McGregor hoeing onions. His back was turned towards Peter, and beyond him was the gate!

Mr. McGregor caught sight of him at the corner, but Peter did not care. He slipped underneath the gate and was safe at last in the wood outside the garden.

Mr. McGregor hung up the little jacket and the shoes for a scare-crow to frighten the blackbirds.

Peter never stopped running or looked behind him till he got home to the big fir-tree.

Character:
Trait:

Record EVIDENCE to help you prove your claim.

Handout 2.3: Finding Text Evidence

The Tale of Peter Rabbit by Beatrix Potter

Name: ______________________________

He was so tired that he flopped down upon the nice soft sand on the floor of the rabbit-hole and shut his eyes. His Mother was busy cooking; she wondered what he had done with his clothes. It was the second little jacket and pair of shoes that Peter had lost in a fortnight!

It was really most provoking for Peter's Mother, because she had not very much money to spend upon new clothes. She earned her living by knitting rabbit-wool mittens and muffettees. I once bought a pair at a bazaar.

She also had a little field in which she grew herbs and rabbit tobacco (this is what we call lavender). She hung it up to dry in the kitchen, in bunches, which she sold for a penny apiece to her rabbit neighbours in the warren.

Did you ever happen to see a little old buck-rabbit enjoying a pipe of rabbit-tobacco?

I am sorry to say that Peter was not very well during the evening in consequence of having eaten too much in Mr. McGregor's garden.

His mother put him to bed and made some chamomile tea; and she gave a dose of it to Peter!

'One table-spoonful to be taken at bed-time.'

But Flopsy, Mopsy, and Cotton-tail had bread and milk and blackberries for supper.

Character:
Trait:

Record EVIDENCE to help you prove your claim.

____
____
____
____
____
____
____
____
____
____
____
____
____
____
____
____
____
____
____
____
____
____
____
____
____
____
____
____
____

TABLE 2.3
Sample Character Trait Evidence

	Peter Rabbit	Mr. McGregor
Clever	Peter gets to a high point in the garden to be able to find his way out.	Mr. McGregor knows how to trap Peter. He also is clearly a clever farmer, as his farm is so successful.
Thoughtful	Peter sits and thinks about how to escape; he also thinks about which animals might be safe to ask for help.	Mr. McGregor is thoughtful in how he tries to trap Peter. He also thinks about what to do with Peter once he traps him.
Careful	Peter knows he must be careful not to get caught. Although he ends up losing it, he is concerned about being careful with his new jacket.	Mr. McGregor tries to find ways to deter animals from coming into his garden. He is also careful not to damage his garden as he pursues Peter.
Responsible	Peter knows that his new clothes are his own responsibility. He is also irresponsible in that he is disobedient and places himself in danger.	Mr. McGregor takes good care of his garden. It is organized and well cared for.
Stubborn	Even though his mother has told him not to go, he makes up his mind to go to the garden. Once he is there, he stubbornly works to get out.	Mr. McGregor is stubborn in his pursuit of Peter.
Tricky	Peter must be tricky to get out of the garden and evade Mr. McGregor.	Mr. McGregor tries to use the element of surprise to capture Peter. He also uses Peter's own clothes as a deterrent to other animals who might enter the garden.

The Socratic Method

- ❑ Requires all students feel safe to contribute to the discussion; team-building must occur before attempting a seminar.
- ❑ Uses questions to examine values and beliefs focusing on moral education as well as information.
- ❑ Demands a classroom environment characterized by "productive discomfort."
- ❑ Is used to demonstrate complexity and uncertainty in our world.

Teacher's Role

- ❏ The teacher is the facilitator. The role of the teacher in a Socratic Seminar shifts from the "Sage on the Stage" to the "Guide on the Side." As the teacher, you must guide the students through further questioning and create a shared dialogue.
- ❏ Find a space where all students can face each other, either moving their desks in a circle or sitting on the floor in a circle.
- ❏ Set dialogue guidelines. Participation requires students to be active listeners. Ask students to connect their statements with those before them using phrases like "I agree with...because..." or "I respectfully disagree with...because..." Remind students that they are encouraged to ask one another questions.
- ❏ Teach students about natural lulls in conversation and when it is appropriate to begin their next statement. Also talk about conversation "hogs" and "logs." A "hog" talks the entire time and doesn't allow others to speak. A "log" is someone who doesn't speak and allows the conversation to take place without their voice.
- ❏ Allow for wait time. Silence is not the enemy! Let students sit with a question for at least 10 seconds without rephrasing it. Students need time to grapple with challenging questions.
- ❏ Encourage students to take ownership of the conversation. Students should ask one another clarifying questions and feel comfortable asking the group a new question to further the discussion.
- ❏ The teacher may interject with either quick teaching moments, clarifying statements, or additional questions; however, this approach should be used with caution so as not to take over the dialogue. See Box 2.3 for some prompting questions to aid with stalls in discussion.

Box 2.3: Socratic Seminar Prompting Questions

- ❏ Who can offer a different perspective?
- ❏ Can you please support that statement with evidence from the text?
- ❏ Can you clarify your statement?
- ❏ Who hasn't had a chance to speak yet?
- ❏ Has anyone had a change of heart?
- ❏ Who has changed their point of view?

- ❏ What piece of evidence made you change your opinion?
- ❏ Can anyone give a counterargument?
- ❏ How can you relate this to your own life?
- ❏ Who else should read this piece? Why?
- ❏ Why is this information important?
- ❏ Do you agree or disagree with the author?
- ❏ What other evidence would you need to change your mind?
- ❏ What else can you tell us about...?
- ❏ What makes you say/think...?

Implementation

- ❏ Go over Socratic Seminar guidelines and expectations. See Box 2.4.

Box 2.4: Socratic Seminar Expectations

- ❏ *All participants must come prepared.*
  - ■ Read the text(s) carefully.
  - ■ Take notes.
  - ■ Complete the Preparation Page.
- ❏ *Be an active participant and listener.*
  - ■ Listen to what others say and don't interrupt.
  - ■ Try to connect your idea to others.
  - ■ "I agree with...because..."
  - ■ "I respectfully disagree with...because..."
  - ■ Ask clarifying questions when needed.
- ❏ *Speak clearly.*
  - ■ State your opinion or idea in concise language.
  - ■ Provide text evidence when possible.
  - ■ Speak at a volume that works for our space and our group.
- ❏ *Be respectful.*
  - ■ Speak only when it is your turn.
  - ■ You don't have to raise your hand, but try not to interrupt others.
  - ■ This is an exchange of ideas, not a debate.

- ❑ Allow students time to prepare. Distribute the Socratic Seminar Graphic Organizer (Handout 2.4) and allow students time to jot down their notes/ideas in the "I think...because..." section. Tell students they will have 10–15 minutes to gather their thoughts on the focus question: "What kind of person/character is ____?" Remind students that the claim they should begin the seminar with should be the one they were given as they read through the story based on their dice rolls.
- ❑ Facilitate the Socratic Seminar. For this exercise, begin with students discussing one character (either Mr. McGregor or Peter). Pose the focus question: "What kind of person/character is ____?" Allow students to share their insights and discuss. Students not actively involved in the discussion should listen attentively and try to form their own opinions based on what the discussion group has to say. As the conversation comes to a natural lull (10–15 minutes), guide students to conclude their seminar, and then switch groups. The second discussion group should focus on the other character (either Mr. McGregor or Peter), and the first discussion group should listen attentively and try to form their own opinions.
- ❑ After the seminar, provide a debrief of what you heard throughout the conversation. Summarize the main points to ensure learning. Finally, have students complete the final section on the Socratic Seminar Preparation Guide (Handout 2.4).
- ❑ **Assessment:** Overall performance and deep thinking based on discussion participation and student thinking framework responses should be informally assessed throughout the unit. Rubrics are available in Appendix A.
    - ■ **Socratic Seminar Rubric:** Quickly assess student participation and preparedness along a continuum to show growth.
    - ■ **Socratic Seminar Self-Reflection:** Students evaluate their own participation and levels of thinking through the seminar process.
- ❑ As a whole group, discuss the following: Which traits were best supported? Why? What made our claims strong? What could have made them stronger? What do we think about each character now?

Handout 2.4: Socratic Seminar Preparation

Name: ______________________________

The question for our Socratic Seminar discussion is:

Find evidence to support your thinking about this question.

EVIDENCE

EVIDENCE

EVIDENCE

Other points I want to raise:

My own opinions:

After our discussion, I think:

Using Evidence Lesson 2: Verifying Claims with Evidence

Objective: Gather evidence to verify and justify a conclusion.

Materials

- ❑ *The Stranger* by Chris Van Allsburg (teacher's copy)
- ❑ Handout 2.5: Read Aloud Reflection (one per student)
- ❑ Individual whiteboards (optional) or scratch paper for each student
- ❑ Handout 2.6: Evidence in Poetry (one per student)

Whole Group Introduction

- ❑ Distribute either individual whiteboards or scratch paper to students. Tell them that you'll be describing some mystery animals, and they should listen for evidence to try and guess each animal. When they have a guess, they should draw or write their guess on their board/paper.
- ❑ Describe the four mystery animals, reading slowly through the prompts and repeating them carefully. Give students time to think and respond, drawing or writing their guesses on their boards/papers.
- ❑ Encourage students as they complete their guesses to jot down key pieces of evidence that helped them determine their answers.
- ❑ Prompts:
  - ■ I am a creature who lives in salt water. I am one of the largest creatures on earth! I love to eat small plankton and krill, and if you're lucky, you might see me come up for air. *(whale)*
  - ■ I am a mammal and I love to hang out in trees. You can spot me if you look closely, but I don't like to make a scene—I spend most of my day sleeping, and when I'm awake I'm a pretty slow mover. I have long claws, and I use my three toes to help me gather leaves to eat. *(sloth)*
  - ■ I am a nocturnal mammal. I use echolocation to find my food. Some people are afraid of me because some of my species share a name with a famous Count, but I only eat bugs and fruit. If you look up at dusk, you can see me and my friends out for our evening snack! *(bat)*
  - ■ I am an amphibian that lives near the pond. I have a long tongue that I use to help me catch insects for my meals. My powerful back

legs help me to jump fast and far to keep me safe from predators. I start my life entirely in the water with no feet at all, but by the time I'm grown, I spend most of my time on land. *(frog)*

- ❑ Review key evidence in each example with the students. Help them to listen carefully for important items that are clues to their single solution. Remind students that the most effective detectives have evidence to support their claims; otherwise, they are just making guesses.

Read Aloud Activity

- ❑ Introduce the book *The Stranger* to the group. Tell them that they'll have to use their convergent thinking skills to be able to really understand the book. Ask them to look carefully for visual and descriptive evidence as to who the stranger really is.
- ❑ Read slowly, thinking aloud as you find potential clues as to who the stranger might be. Point out how things change in the illustrations, as well as strange actions/events that might make us wonder.
- ❑ After reading, go through the Read Aloud Reflection page (Handout 2.5) together. Encourage and support students to accurately name their thinking processes as they work through the page. For Key Understandings, see Box 2.5. In the end, they'll use evidence from the book to come up with a conclusion about the characters.

Box 2.5: *The Stranger*: Key Understandings

- ❑ *Story summary*: In this beautifully illustrated book, a stranger arrives on a family's farm in late summer. The family takes him in, and somehow, while the season changes to fall in surrounding areas, it remains summer at the Bailey farm. The stranger is perplexed by the lack of changing leaves and other signs of fall on the Bailey farm. One day, he examines a green leaf, blows on it, and has a major realization, remembering who he is. He dons his old clothes and leaves the Bailey farm, which promptly turns seasons to late fall.
- ❑ *Evidence as to the stranger's identity*: The mercury in the doctor's thermometer is stuck at the bottom; the stranger blows on a leaf to change it; cold seems to follow the stranger around; the frost on the Baileys' barn reads, "see you next fall."

Handout 2.5: Read Aloud Reflection

The Stranger by Chris Van Allsburg

Name: ______________________________

Summarize the main idea of the story.

What pieces of evidence point to the identity of the stranger?

What is KNOWN about the stranger?

What is UNKNOWN about the stranger?

What are some details that happen while the stranger is present?

Who do you think the stranger is? Why?

- ❑ *What we know about the stranger*: Cold air seems to follow him. He is fascinated by nature around him.
- ❑ *What is unknown about the stranger*: His name, where he comes from, his identity.
- ❑ *While the stranger is present*: The Bailey farm stays stuck in the present season (summer). Cold air comes in waves, usually when the stranger blows.
- ❑ *Who is the stranger?* Jack Frost! He brings the cooler weather and air that changes the season from summer to fall to winter.

Skill Development Activity

- ❑ Introduce the concept of an extended metaphor to students. Extended metaphor is used when an author makes a comparison of one thing to another. In poetry, this is often done without ever mentioning the theme item being named.
- ❑ Give an example. Read aloud "Fog" by Carl Sandburg.

Box 2.6: "Fog" by Carl Sandburg, 1916

The fog comes in
on little cat feet.

It sits looking
over a harbor and a city
on silent haunches
and then moves on.

- ❑ Discuss the poem. As questions such as: What is being compared? How is the fog like a cat? Point out that although a cat and fog may seem very different, the fact that Sandburg compares one to the other seems to make sense. This makes his poem an effective metaphor—even though we understand that the comparison is of very different items, we can also visualize the similarity because of the way they are described.

- ❑ Tell students that today they will be working with another poem by the African American writer Alice Dunbar Nelson. Nelson was famous for writing both poetry and prose and lived from 1875 to 1935. Today, students will be reading one of her poems called "Impressions." In this poem, Nelson wrote about five abstract concepts: faith, thought, hope, love, and death. She describes her "impressions" of each in a single stanza.
- ❑ Distribute Handout 2.6a to students. On this page, students will see each of the five stanzas of Nelson's poem "Impressions." Working individually or with a partner, students will read each stanza and try to find evidence to determine which concept the stanza is referencing. Students will cut apart the stanza titles at the bottom of the handout and glue them next to the appropriate stanzas in the poem, and then they will describe the evidence from the stanza that brought them to their conclusions. *(Solutions, from top to bottom: thought, hope, love, death, faith)*
- ❑ Discuss the activity as a whole group. What evidence helped students match the titles with the stanzas?
- ❑ Distribute Handout 2.6b to students. Tell them that now it is their turn to create a mystery poem. For this exercise, they'll be creating a special kind of poem called a diamante. In this format, students will choose a topic (noun) to be the theme of their poem. They will brainstorm words that relate to their theme, and then they will craft the seven-line poem using the provided template on the handout. For this poem, students will not use the theme word of their poem anywhere in the template—they should keep this a mystery. The template consists of a mirrored outline: lines 1 and 7 are synonyms of the theme; lines 2 and 6 each consist of two adjectives describing the theme; lines 3 and 5 each consist of three *-ing* verbs (gerunds) related to the theme; and line 4 consists of four nouns/emotions related to the theme.
- ❑ Give students time to independently craft their diamante poems. Circulate and support students' work as needed.
- ❑ Once students have completed their poems, invite students to read their poems aloud, either for a partner, a small group, or the class. As each poem is shared, the other students should listen attentively for evidence that will reveal the theme of the poem. Once the poem has been read, elicit student guesses as to the theme of the poem. Each guess should be accompanied by supporting evidence from the poem. Emphasize the importance of finding valid evidence to support each claim.
- ❑ Display student-created poems if possible.

Handout 2.6a: Evidence in Poetry

Name: ______________________________

Match the title with each stanza of Alice Dunbar Nelson's poem, "Impressions". Then, make notes of the evidence in the poem that you used to make each match.

A swift, successive chain of things, That flash, kaleidoscope-like, now in, now out, Now straight, now eddying in wild rings, No order, neither law, compels their moves, But endless, constant, always swiftly roves.	GLUE STANZA TITLE HERE	EVIDENCE:
Wild seas of tossing, writhing waves, A wreck half-sinking in the tortuous gloom; One man clings desperately, while Boreas raves, And helps to blot the rays of moon and star, Then comes a sudden flash of light, which gleams on shores afar.	GLUE STANZA TITLE HERE	EVIDENCE:
A bed of roses, pleasing to the eye, Flowers of heaven, passionate and pure, Upon this bed the youthful often lie, And pressing hard upon its sweet delight, The cruel thorns pierce soul and heart, and cause a woeful blight.	GLUE STANZA TITLE HERE	EVIDENCE:
A traveler who has always heard That on this journey he some day must go, Yet shudders now, when at the fatal word He starts upon the lonesome, dreary way. The past, a page of joy and woe,—the future, none can say.	GLUE STANZA TITLE HERE	EVIDENCE:
Blind clinging to a stern, stone cross, Or it may be of frailer make; Eyes shut, ears closed to earth's drear dross, Immovable, serene, the world away From thoughts—the mind uncaring for another day.	GLUE STANZA TITLE HERE	EVIDENCE:

LOVE	**DEATH**	**HOPE**	**FAITH**	**THOUGHT**

Handout 2.6b: Evidence in Poetry

Name: ______________________________

Now it's your turn to create a poem that your friends can draw evidence from. For this exercise, you'll be writing a diamante poem. Using a topic (noun) of your choosing, you'll craft the poem using the template. Then, you'll share your poem with the group, asking them to listen for evidence as to the subject of your poem.

First, create a word web. Place your topic in the center, and then think of as many adjectives, synonyms, verbs, and connected feelings for your topic as you can.

Now, use the ideas you generated above to fill in the template and complete your poem.

SYNONYM

ADJECTIVE | ADJECTIVE

-ING VERB | -ING VERB | -ING VERB

RELATED NOUN/FEELING | RELATED NOUN/FEELING | RELATED NOUN/FEELING | RELATED NOUN/FEELING

-ING VERB | -ING VERB | -ING VERB

ADJECTIVE | ADJECTIVE

ANOTHER SYNONYM

Using Evidence Authentic Application Activity: Validating Solutions with Evidence

Objective: Gather evidence from a variety of sources and apply evidence to possible solutions in order to make a substantiated claim.

Materials

- ❑ *Seven Blind Mice* by Ed Young (teacher's copy)
- ❑ Handout 2.7: Read Aloud Reflection (one per student)
- ❑ Handout 2.8.a–d: Island Fact Sheets (four pages, either enlarged for whole-class viewing or duplicated, one set per small group of students)
- ❑ Handout 2.9.a–f: Hidden Treasure Clues (six pages, one set per student)
- ❑ Handout 2.10: Hidden Treasure Recording Sheet (one per student)

Whole Group Introduction

- ❑ Engage students in a brief discussion about evidence. Use questions such as the following:
  - ■ Where can evidence be found?
  - ■ How do we know if evidence is valid?
  - ■ What is a red herring? (You may need to define this term for students as something that draws attention away from the accurate solution.)
- ❑ Remind students that in order to make justifiable solutions, they must gather all the information they can, and put it together to find a solution.
- ❑ Demonstrate the need for gathering evidence. Gather a stack of paper consisting of two or three colors shuffled together. Ask the students what they notice (that there are multiple colors). Ask them to consider the following: If I needed 12 sheets of (single color) paper for a project, could we determine if I have enough right here using only observation? We could not. In order to find a solution (is there enough of a color for my project?), we would need to find evidence by counting and organize our information so that we can be sure of our solution.

Read Aloud Activity

- ❑ Distribute the *Seven Blind Mice* Read Aloud Reflection page (Handout 2.7). Students will use this page to follow along with the read aloud.

Handout 2.7: Read Aloud Reflection

Seven Blind Mice by Ed Young

Name: ______________________________

As the story is read, sketch what each mouse "saw".

Red Mouse	Green Mouse	Yellow Mouse

Purple Mouse	Orange Mouse	Blue Mouse

Before the final page, predict: What is the object?	What did White Mouse see? Were you correct?

What evidence did each mouse use to support his claim?	How did the solution change once all the evidence had been gathered together?

- ❏ Read aloud the story *Seven Blind Mice* by Ed Young *without showing any pictures*. As you read, stop at each page, and allow students to think about and infer what each mouse is "seeing." Pause and allow time for students to fill in their thoughts on the reflection page. See Box 2.7 for Key Understandings.
- ❏ After you complete reading the story one time without pictures, ask students to flip their page over and draw the story again, this time as you read through while showing pictures. Have them draw the elephant, piece by piece, drawing each part that the mice see in order.
- ❏ Allow students to complete the two reflection questions at the end, and then discuss this story and activity as a whole group. Emphasize the point that although each mouse had its own evidence, we needed all of the pieces together in order to have a correct solution.

Box 2.7: Seven Blind Mice Key Understandings

- ❏ *Story summary*: Seven blind mice find an object. One at a time, they approach the object, each examining a different portion object and each returning to the group drawing a different conclusion about what the object might be. Finally, the seventh mouse determines that each mouse has been incorrect because each mouse has only felt one part of the object. The whole object is revealed—it's an elephant.
- ❏ *Each mouse's perspective*:
  - ■ Red: a pillar (the elephant's foot)
  - ■ Green: a snake (the elephant's trunk)
  - ■ Yellow: a spear (the elephant's tusk)
  - ■ Purple: a cliff (the top of the elephant's head)
  - ■ Orange: a fan (the elephant's ear)
  - ■ Blue: a rope (the elephant's tail)
  - ■ White: an elephant (the whole elephant)
- ❏ *Evidence*: Each mouse used their sense of touch to draw a conclusion based on only the portion of the elephant they examined.
- ❏ *Change in the final solution*: Each part of the elephant was, indeed, as described by each individual mouse. It was only once all the pieces were put together that the entire solution could become apparent.

Authentic Application Lesson

- ❑ Prepare the activity.
  - ■ Reproduce the Island Fact Sheets (Handout 2.8.a–d). This can be done either by enlarging each to a size that can be viewed by multiple students at once in a gallery walk, or by creating one set of fact sheets (four in total) for each small group.
  - ■ Duplicate the six Treasure Hunt Clues (Handout 2.9.a–), so that each student or small group has their own copy of each clue.
  - ■ Place the clues at various spots throughout the classroom (one clue in each location) to allow students to move from clue to clue.
  - ■ Reproduce the Treasure Hunt Recording Sheet (Handout 2.10) for each student.
- ❑ Set the scene for students: Captain Dreadful and his band of pirates need your help. They've buried all their treasure on an island in the Caribbean to keep it safe from other rival pirate gangs. Problem is, now they can't remember which one! You need to gather evidence to help them remember which island has their treasure. Be sure to base your guesses on evidence—if you're wrong, the pirates will make you walk the plank!
- ❑ Divide students into six small groups that will work collaboratively to solve the clues and find the treasure.
- ❑ Distribute Handout 2.10 (Recording Sheet) to each student. Remind students of the importance of recording evidence as they find it so that they can verify their conclusions. Instruct students that they will be moving around the room with their collaborative groups to find clues. Groups should stay at a clue location until you give the signal to switch positions.
- ❑ Direct groups to a starting station. Each group will begin with a single clue, working to solve the clue at their station. Be sure to alert students as to whether each student should complete a clue page or whether they should complete one clue page as a group, in accordance with how you choose to duplicate clue sheets. Allow groups several minutes to work at their first station, scaffolding support as needed.
- ❑ Ask students to pause their work and give you their attention. Remind students to record the evidence they have learned from their clue on their recording sheet (Handout 2.10).
- ❑ Direct groups to rotate to another clue station and repeat the work process, adjusting timing and support as needed. Students should eventually reach all six stations. See Figures 2.1–2.6 for answer keys to each clue.

CUBA

National Flower: Butterfly Jasmine (white)

Cuba is the largest Caribbean island, and the 17th largest in the world. Its capital is Havana, which is home to amazing architecture and culture. The official language is Spanish, and the most popular sport is baseball. Its population is about 11 million. Cuba gained independence from Spain in 1902, and it has been an independent republic ever since.

"Pearl of the Antilles"

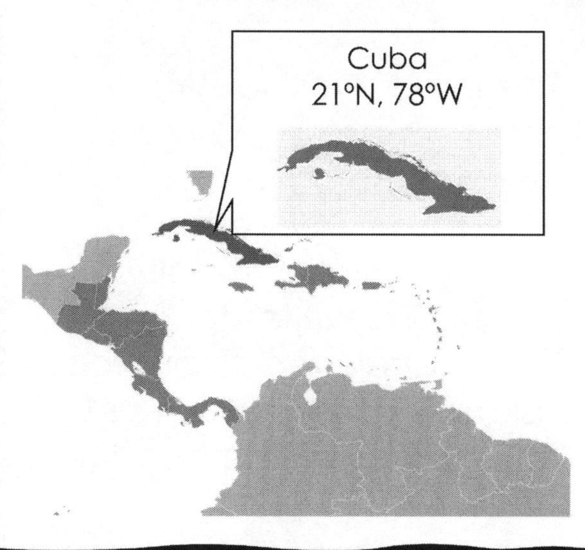

The flag of Cuba is tricolored. Alternating blue and white stripes and a white star on an equilateral red triangle symbolize the ideals of liberty, equality, and brotherhood. The star symbolizes the independence of Cuba.

PUERTO RICO

National Flower:
Flor de Maga
(pink)

Puerto Rico is a territory of the United States of America but has previously been under Spanish rule. While it is not a state, statehood for Puerto Rico has been a topic of debate for quite some time. Spanish and English are both national languages. Puerto Rico is known for its beautiful beaches and Spanish-Caribbean culture with an American flair.

"Island of Enchantment"

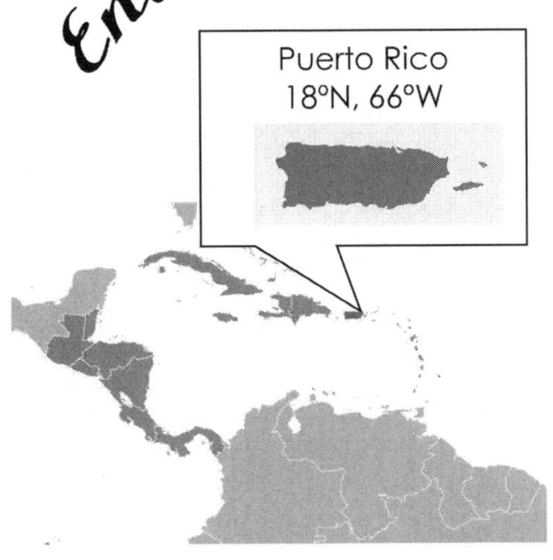

The three red stripes on the flag symbolize the brave warriors who have fought for Puerto Rico, while the two white stripes symbolize peace. The white star on the blue triangle represents the island's placement in the blue waters of the ocean.

BARBADOS

National Flower:
Pride of Barbados/
Peacock Flower
(red/orange)

Barbados is a small island in the Caribbean that is renowned for its friendly local inhabitants. It is an English-speaking parliamentary republic, and its population is about 285,000 people. Its capital is Bridgetown, a vibrant and historic city. The west and south sides of the island are known for their beaches, while the eastern coast is made up of rugged cliffs.

"Pride and Industry"

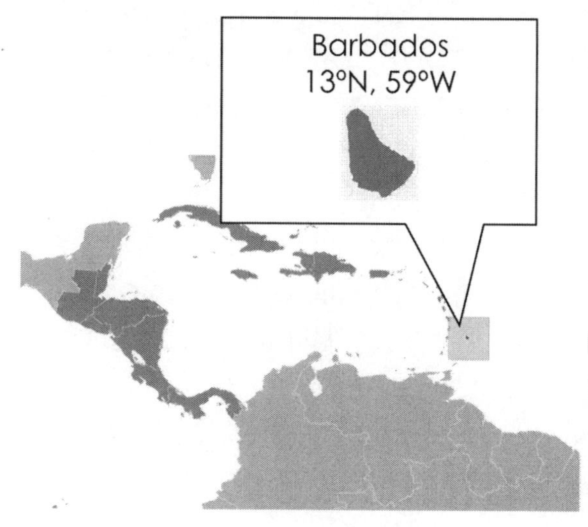

Barbados is famous in pirate lore, and its flag represents its location. The two outer blue stripes represent the sea and sky of Barbados. The gold stripe in the center represents the beaches. The trident in the center is a nod to Neptune, the Roman god of the sea.

JAMAICA

National Flower: Lignum Vitae (purple)

Jamaica is the third largest Caribbean island, and its name means "Land of Wood and Water". Its capital is Kingston, which is on the southern end of the island. The official language is English, although most locals speak the patois dialect. Its population is about 2.5 million people and it gained independence from Great Britain in 1962.

"Out of Many, One People"

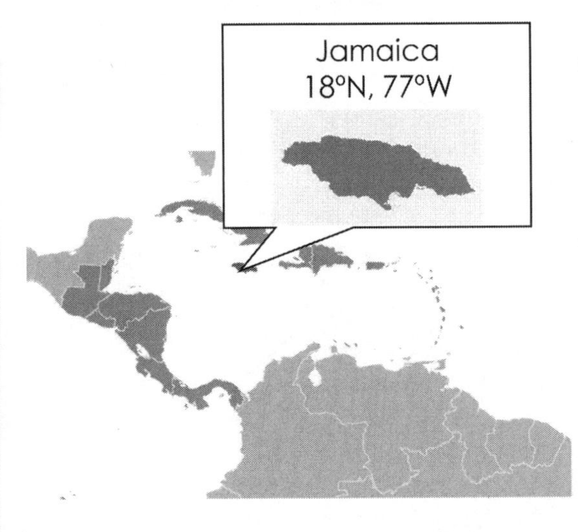

Jamaica is a major tourist destination and has a rich and vibrant culture. The colors on the flag represent the strength of the people (black triangles on left and right), the wealth of the country and the sunshine (yellow diagonal cross), and the lush green vegetation on the island, as well as hope (green triangles on top and bottom).

Handout 2.9a: Hidden Treasure Clues

CLUE 1

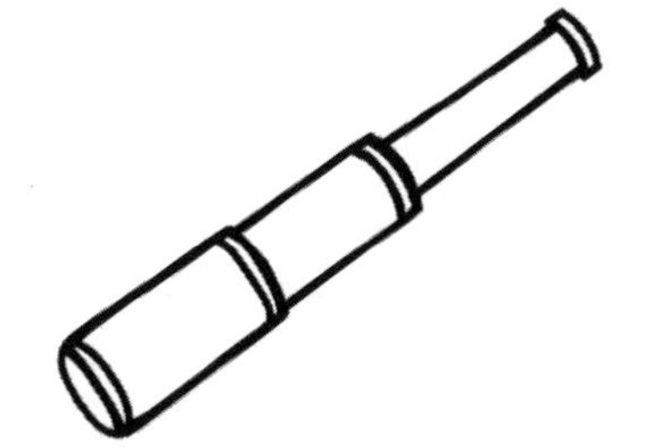

Key:

1. Shade all numbers divisible by 2 blue.
2. Shade all number divisible by 3 green.
3. Shade all numbers divisible by 5 purple.
4. Shade all remaining numbers yellow.

20	99	42	8	24	39	4	82	70
14	50	88	66	35	45	10	94	55
33	1	17	79	90	7	19	59	22
15	27	12	83	84	41	20	61	40
62	13	11	19	36	53	71	97	28
21	37	36	54	48	67	84	89	56
90	79	47	23	65	29	75	13	75
85	6	10	25	72	9	26	85	8
18	14	74	92	40	16	78	60	12

Those yellow "stars" are pointing our ship somewhere...what constellation do we see? What clue did you uncover?

SUPPORT MATERIAL

CLUE 2

Sort these colors into the Venn Diagram.

purple	gold	violet	bronze	white
orange	yellow	blue	black	gray
pink	silver	indigo	red	green

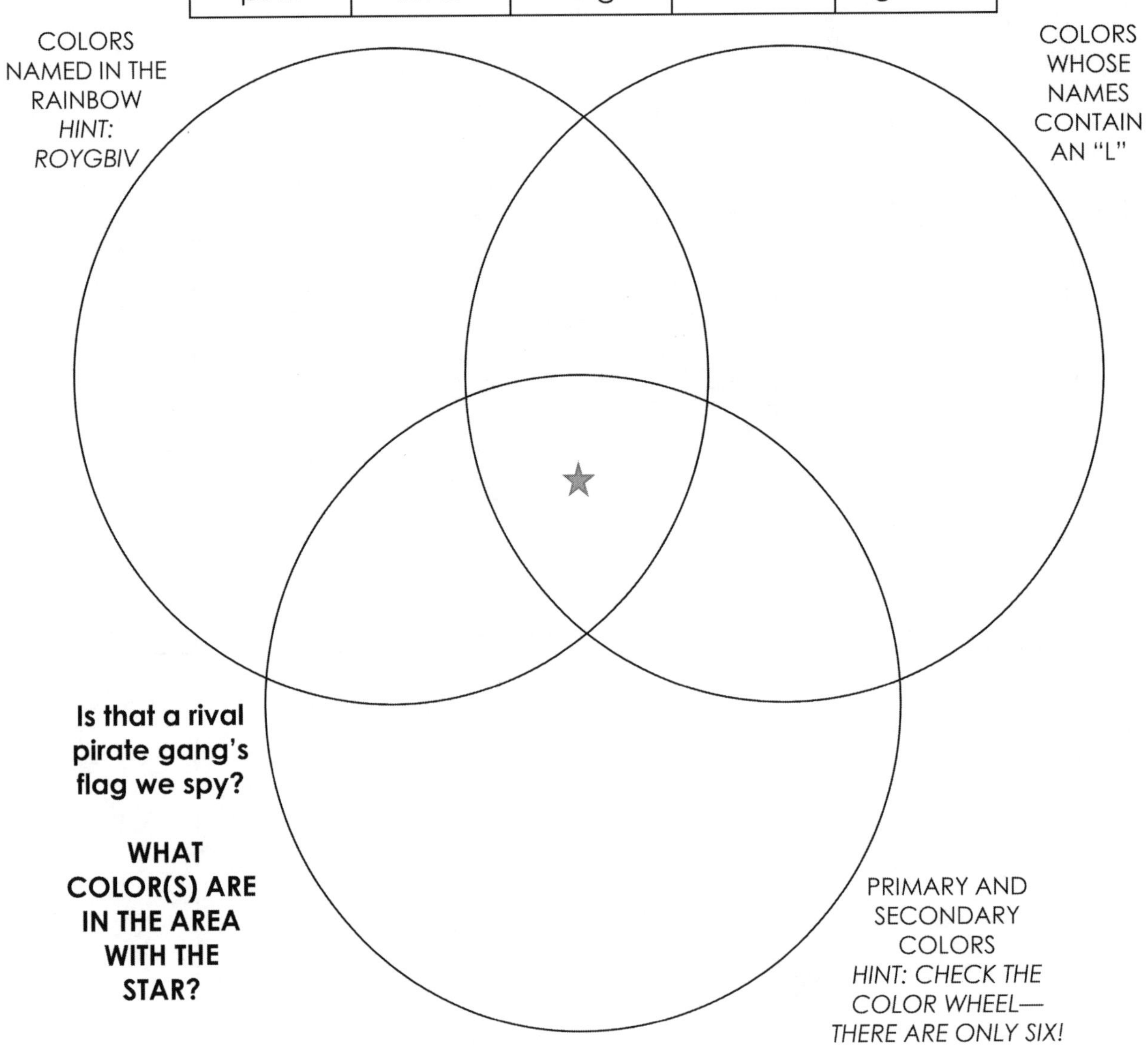

Is that a rival pirate gang's flag we spy?

WHAT COLOR(S) ARE IN THE AREA WITH THE STAR?

Handout 2.9c: Hidden Treasure Clues

CLUE 3

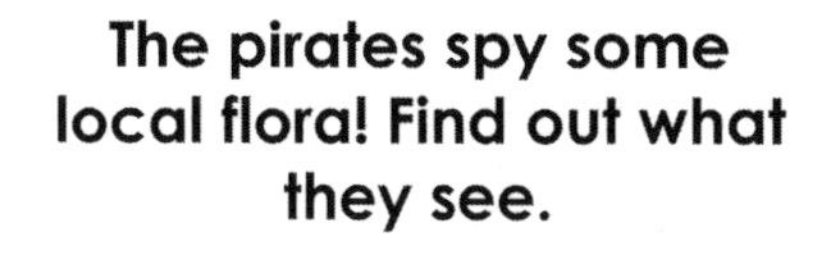

The pirates spy some local flora! Find out what they see.

Moving from the top of the tower to the bottom, create a path down the tower which adds up to 55. Your path must move in a downward direction, and you may only move into new blocks which are touching the block you are moving out of. When you reach the bottom, follow the path from your ending point to the clue!

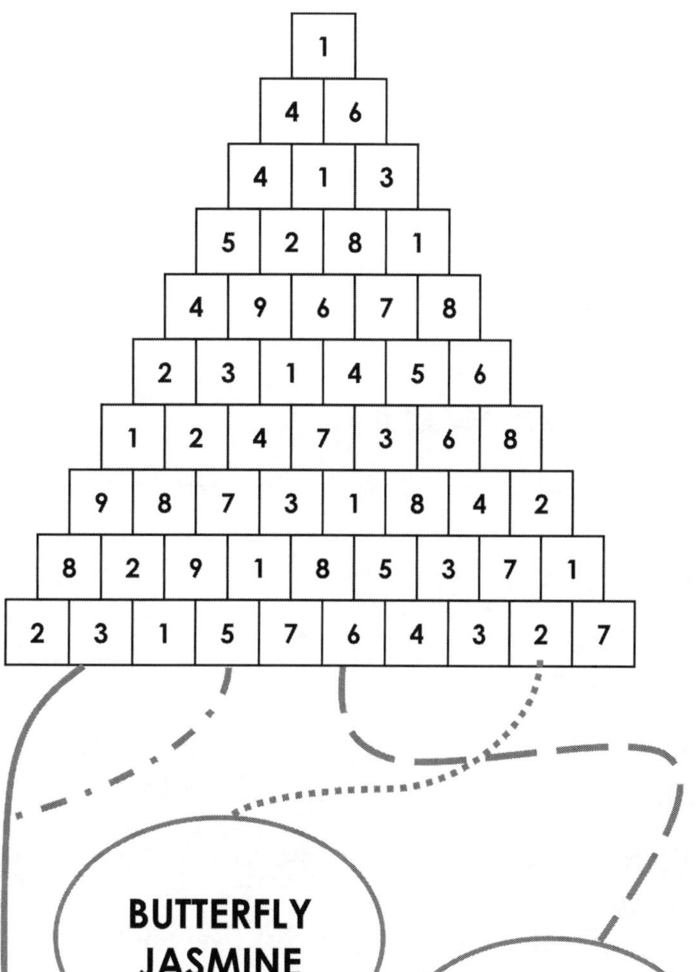

CLUE 4

A message in the sand! Solve the riddles. Then, crack the pirate's code by matching the numbers in your answers to the letter of the question in the grid below to reveal your clue.

M. The number of inches in a foot: ______

D. The number of days in two weeks: ______

B. The number of pennies in a dollar: ______

A. The number of letters in the third month of the year: _____

R. The number of cups in a gallon: _______

H. The number of cards in a standard deck: ______

O. The number of minutes in an hour: ______

I. The number of feet in a yard: _______

L. The number of days in October: _______

N. The number of pounds in a ton: _______

G. The number of innings in a baseball game: _______

J. The number of colors in the rainbow: _______

P. The number of letters in the alphabet: _______

E. The number of bagels in a baker's dozen: _______

U. The number of states in the United States of America: _______

16	13	14	52	13	16	16	3	2000	9

CLUE 5

The captain of the ship bought five of her pirates a new eye patch, which cost three gold pieces each. If she handed the cashier a coin worth 20 gold pieces, how much change should she receive?

Longbeard's pet parrot, Polly, knows 3 times as many words as Captain Dreadful's pet parrot, Petey. Polly knew 7 words last week, but she just learned two more. How many words does Petey know?

Usually, the Perilous Pirates have twelve sea routes they can use to get back to their buried treasure. Sadly, five are currently blocked by rival pirate gangs. Another half a dozen routes are blocked because it's low tide. How many routes are still open for the pirates?

Each pirate ship needs three sails raised in order to sail. They have already raised 12 and have enough sail fabric to raise 17 more. How many ships will they be able to sail?

SUPPORT MATERIAL

CLUE 6

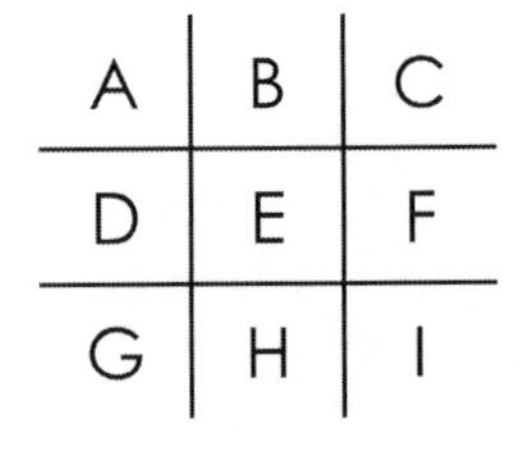

J K L
M N O
P Q R

The pirates found this coded message in the lower deck of the ship. Use the code to solve it before they make you walk the plank!

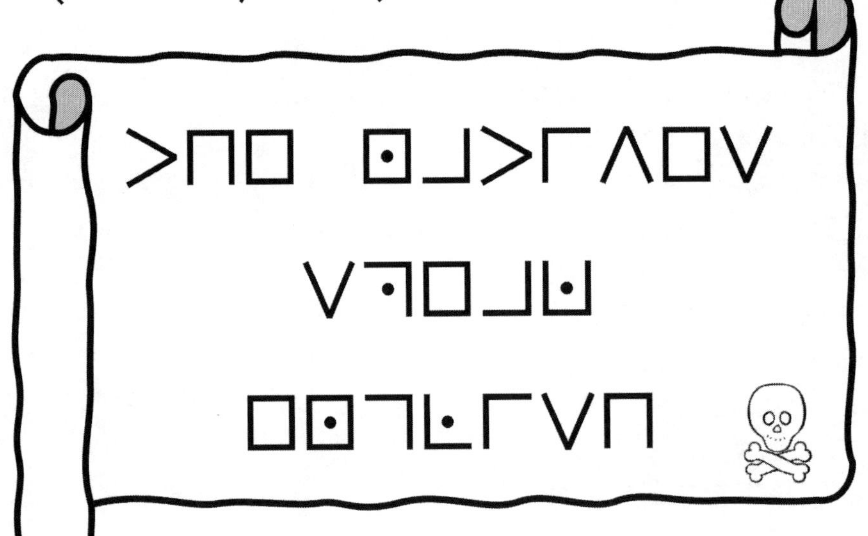

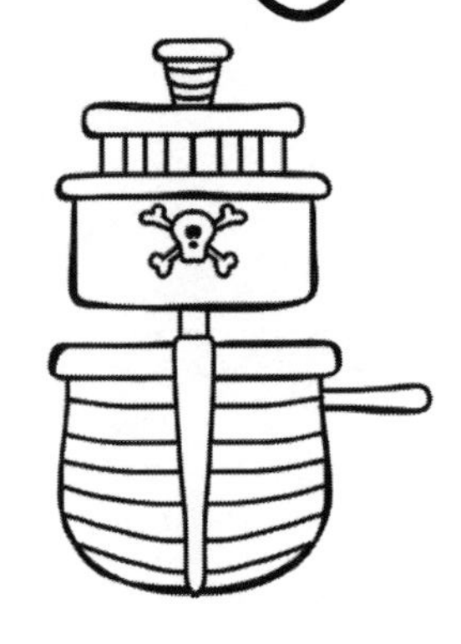

Handout 2.10: Hidden Treasure Recording Sheet

RECORDING SHEET

I think the buried treasure is located on:

____

CLUE	Evidence: What did we learn?	Reasoning: how does this support my claim (solution)?
1		
2		
3		
4		
5		
6		

Reflect on this activity. How did the evidence help you determine your solution?

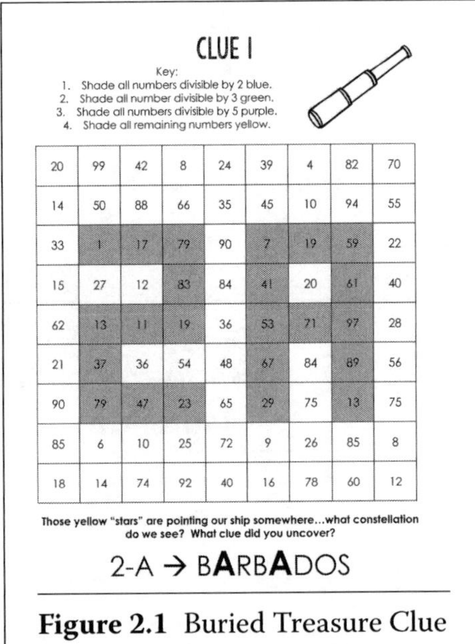

Figure 2.1 Buried Treasure Clue #1 Answer Key

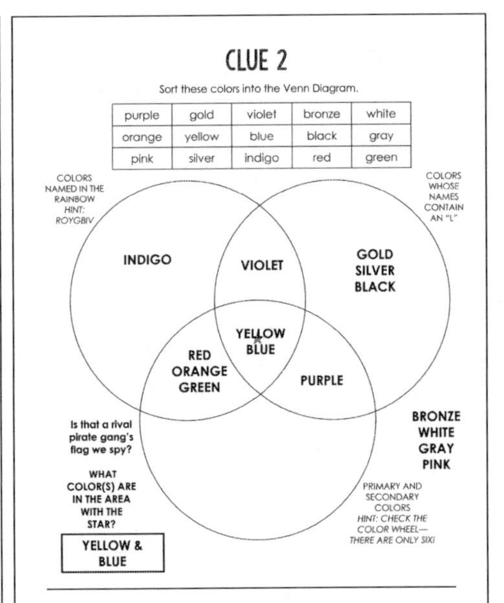

Figure 2.2 Buried Treasure Clue #2 Answer Key

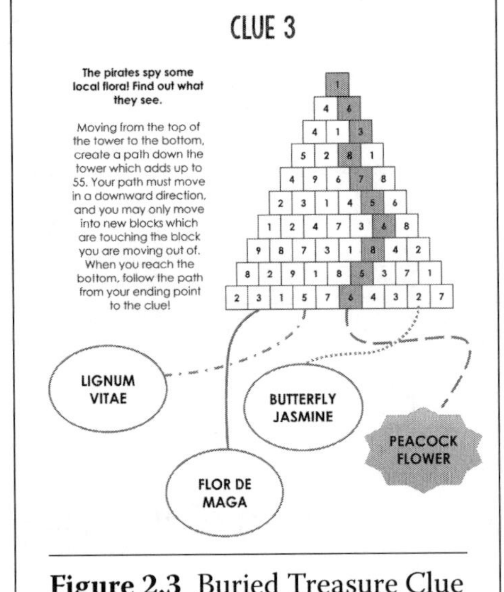

Figure 2.3 Buried Treasure Clue #3 Answer Key

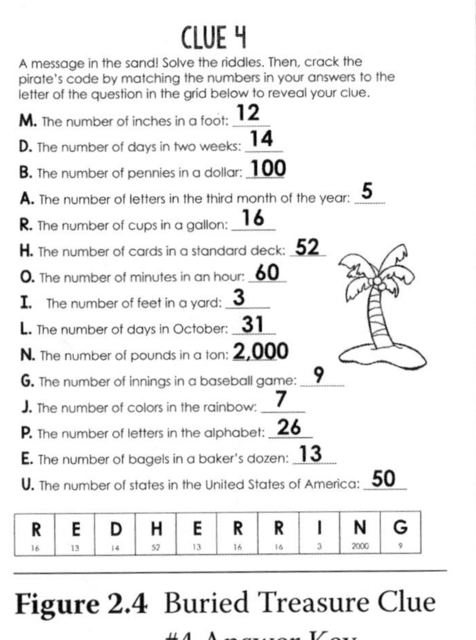

Figure 2.4 Buried Treasure Clue #4 Answer Key

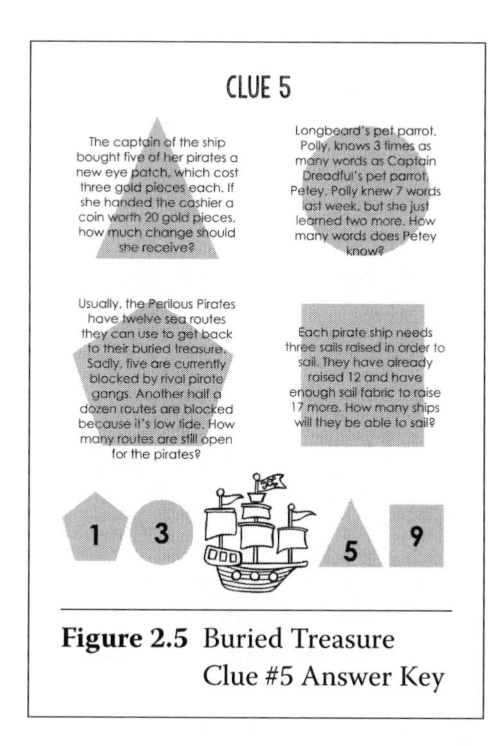

Figure 2.5 Buried Treasure Clue #5 Answer Key

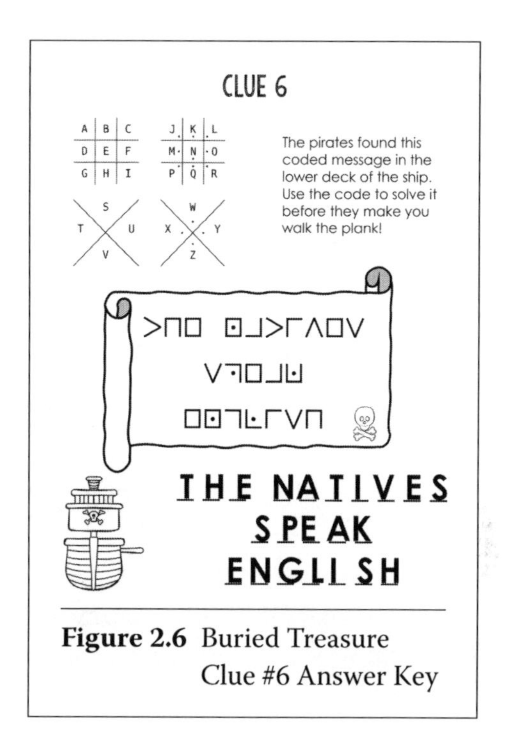

Figure 2.6 Buried Treasure Clue #6 Answer Key

- ❑ Once students have completed all six stations, bring the group back together. As a whole group, direct students to work with the Island Fact Sheets (Handout 2.8.a–d) to try and discover where the treasure is hidden. This can be done using either a gallery walk or small group copies. Students will need to be able to read and consider each of the Island Fact Sheets (Handouts 2.8.a–d).
  - Gallery Walk: Students will physically walk between enlarged versions of the island fact sheets, trying to match their evidence to one of the islands.
  - Small Groups: Each student group receives a copy of each of the island fact sheets, and students collaboratively discuss evidence to determine which island holds the treasure.
- ❑ Once students are able to claim a solution, discuss as a whole group. What clues helped? How did you rule out certain islands? Were some clues more/less helpful than others?

Using Evidence Concluding Activities

- ❑ Distribute the Using Evidence Exit Ticket (Appendix A). Ask students to reflect on their learning about the skill of using evidence to make and verify claims. Allow time for students to complete the exit ticket. Use this as a formative assessment, to gain a better understanding of your students' readiness to effectively practice the skill of using evidence.

- ❏ If desired, complete the Group Using Evidence Rubric (Appendix A) to track students' progress with the skill.
- ❏ If desired, use the Convergent Thinking Student Observation Rubric (Appendix A) to assess and quantify individual students' mastery.
- ❏ Ask students to retrieve their Convergent Thinking Avatar (Handout I.3). In the Using Evidence box, they should either record the main ideas about the thinking skill or illustrate their avatar using the skill of using evidence.

Bibliography

Evans, J. (n.d.). CC BY-SA 4.0. <https://creativecommons.org/licenses/by-sa/4.0>, via Wikimedia Commons. https://upload.wikimedia.org/wikipedia/commons/e/e6/Peacock_Flower_or_Pride-of-Barbados_--_Caesalpinia_pulcherrima.jpg.

Fog (n.d.). Poetry.com. https://www.poetry.com/poem/4664/fog.

Higgins, R.T. (2015). *Mother Bruce.* Los Angeles, CA: Disney-Hyperion.

https://www.flickr.com/photos/oquendo/4612691714/CC BY 2.0.

Impressions. (n.d.). https://allpoetry.com/Impressions.

Potter, B. (2002). *The tale of Peter Rabbit.* London: Warne.

Starr, F. and Starr, K. (n.d.). CC BY 3.0 <https://creativecommons.org/licenses/by/3.0>, via Wikimedia Commons. https://upload.wikimedia.org/wikipedia/commons/b/b9/Starr_070727-7629_Guaiacum_officinale.jpg.

Van Allsburg, C. (1986). *The stranger.* Boston, MA: HMH Books for Young Readers.

Vijayanrajapuram. (n.d.). CC BY-SA 4.0. <https://creativecommons.org/licenses/by-sa/4.0>, via Wikimedia Commons https://upload.wikimedia.org/wikipedia/commons/7/7c/Hedychium_coronarium_white_ginger_lily_vijayanrajapuram.jpg.

The World Factbook. (2021). Washington, DC: Central Intelligence Agency, 2021. https://www.cia.gov/the-world-factbook/.

Young, E. (2002). *Seven blind mice.* New York: Puffin Books.

CHAPTER 3

Sub-Skill 3

Inferencing

TABLE 3.1
Inferencing Sub-Skill Overview

Thinking Skill Outline	
Focus Questions	❏ How can we use our observations and schema to make predictions? ❏ What information is missing? Can we make a guess to fill some of the gaps?
Lesson 1	*Using Observations to Infer* ❏ **Trade Book Focus:** *Who What Where?* by Olivier Tallec ❏ **Practice Activity:** "The Box." Students will watch an animated short film and make inferences about the characters and theme based on what they see.
Lesson 2	*Missing Information* ❏ **Trade Book Focus:** *This Is Not My Hat* by Jon Klassen ❏ **Practice Activity:** "What's the Story?" Students will work with an interesting scene to make inferences and write a story. They will conclude with an inferencing "I Have, Who Has?" game.
Authentic Application Activity	*Shipwreck Scenario* ❏ **Practice Activity:** A shipwreck has left suitcases and passengers' belongings littered across the beach. Using inferencing, can you return the belongings to each passenger? This activity is presented with three levels of challenge for easy differentiation.

DOI: 10.4324/9781003268307-4

Inferencing Lesson 1: Using Observations to Infer

Objective: Develop skills in making inferences based upon visual clues.

Materials

- ❑ *Who, What, Where?* by Olivier Tallec (teacher's copy)
- ❑ Handout 3.2: Read Aloud Reflection (one per student)
- ❑ *Optional:* Handout 3.3: Who, What, Where? Puzzle Template (one per student or partnership)
- ❑ Handout 3.4: Visual Inferencing Worksheet
- ❑ Device to display short video clip: "The Box"/"*La Boîte*" by ESMA
  - Video clip available at: https://youtu.be/20evunLzSgk
  - *Teacher's note*: Be sure you have the correct video. There are several videos titled "The Box" on YouTube; the correct video is posted by CGMeetup channel.

Whole Group Introduction

- ❑ Introduce the skill of *inferencing* to the students. Show the Inferencing Anchor Chart poster (Handout 3.1) to them, pointing out that inferencing means using what we know to make educated guesses about what we don't know.
- ❑ Write the following pattern on the board: 2, 4, 6, ____, 10. Ask the students to *infer* what number is missing. Ask how they found their answer. Lead the discussion to the fact that students had both background knowledge (how to count by twos) and visual cues (the numbers they could see) as evidence to fill in the missing part. Repeat a couple more times using other number patterns (counting by fives, decreasing by threes, multiplying by fours, etc.), emphasizing that students must use both what they know and what they can see in order to make an inference.

Handout 3.1: Inferencing Anchor Chart

Read Aloud Activity

- ❑ Introduce the book to students by telling them that they will use visual clues to *infer* who each riddle is referring to. Remind them that to make a valid *inference*, they will need to have evidence to back up their claims!
- ❑ Read the book together. Model the process of inferencing using the first page, thinking aloud to explicitly show thinking processes involved. Use prompts like "What I *can* see is..." "What I think I'm missing is..." and/or "I know from experience that..."
- ❑ As you read each page and complete each puzzle together as a whole group, ask students to make an inference to find the solution silently, giving a silent signal (such as a thumbs up) to signify that they think they have a solution. Working in this way gives all students time to think before the answer is revealed. Ask students to point out the visual cues they used to make their inferences, providing evidence for their solutions.
- ❑ Distribute the Read Aloud Reflection page (Handout 3.2). Allow students time to reflect on the read aloud, scaffolding support as needed. Emphasize the point that it was visual cues which helped us make inferences in this book, even though the visual clues did not give away the answers fully. For expanded key understandings, see Box 3.1.

Box 3.1: *Who, What, Where?* Key Understandings

- ❑ *Story summary*: This book presents a series of visual puzzles, each asking students which of several choices is the indicated solution.
- ❑ *Connection to inferencing*: Readers must use what they observe in each image along with what they know about the given situation in order to infer which of the "suspects" matches the puzzle description.
- ❑ *Connection to observation*: Readers must observe visual clues carefully—there are several puzzles with suspects who are visually similar, and only one solution is correct on each page.

- ❑ At the end of the Read Aloud Reflection page (Handout 3.2), students are directed to create their own "Who, What, Where?"–style puzzles. If desired, distribute Handout 3.3 to each student (or partner pair, depending on student readiness and interest level) and allow students

Handout 3.2: Read Aloud Reflection

Who What Where? by Olivier Tallec

Name: ______________________________

Give a brief overview of the book.

How did the book force the reader to use inferencing?

Which page(s) were trickiest to infer? Why?

How did this book combine **observation** with **inferring**?

Create your own "Who What Where" riddle for a friend to solve! Be sure to include at least three options for solutions. You can use the template provided if you'd like or create your own. Use this space to plan your riddle, including the question you'll ask and what clues will be included.

Handout 3.3: Who What Where Puzzle Template

Name: ______________________________

Who ______________________________?

to publish their original puzzles. Post these in an area for display so that students may try and solve these peer-written original puzzles.

Skill Development Activity

In this activity, students will be shown an animated short film entitled "The Box"/"*La Boîte*" by ESMA. *Teacher's note*: Be sure you have the correct video. There are several videos titled "The Box" on YouTube; the correct video is posted by CGMeetup channel. The link to the correct video is provided in the "Materials" section of this lesson.

- ❑ In this wordless short, a man interacts with a mouse in his home. The characters display a wide range of emotions and actions that demonstrate how their feelings change over time.
- ❑ Distribute Handout 3.4 to students before showing the video clip.
- ❑ The first time you show the video, stop at the times indicated on the activity sheet (1:00, 2:00, 3:00, 4:30, and 6:30) to discuss what inferences can be made based on visual cues. Ask students to record both their inferences as well as their reasoning in the table. See Box 3.2 for key understandings to target on Handout 3.4.

Box 3.2: Key Understandings for Handout 3.4, Visual Inferencing

Time	Inference	Reasoning
1:00	The man is trying to trap a mouse.	The man is hiding from the mouse but is clearly watching it at the same time.
2:00	The man does not like mice. He might be afraid of them.	He is very excited to have trapped the mouse under the box, and finally comes out of his hiding spot.
3:00	The man does not want the mouse in his house, but he is unsure what to do with it. He feels like he can't just let it go.	Even though he was excited to trap the mouse, he now looks very concerned. He thinks about putting the mouse outside, but decides against it.
4:30	The mouse is curious; it does not seem to be afraid.	It moves around within the box, looks around itself, and tosses the crumbs back to the man.
6:30	The man and the mouse learn to trust and care for one another.	Their interactions grow closer together, and their facial expressions show trust.

Handout 3.4: Visual Inferencing

Name: ______________________________

Watch the animated short "The Box". Pause at the times listed below to record your inferences. Then, watch the short film again to see the whole thing without pausing. Complete the reflection questions.

TIME	INFERENCE	REASONING
1:00	What is happening here?	
2:00	What are the man's feelings about the mouse?	
3:00	What has changed?	
4:30	What are the mouse's feelings?	
6:30	How can you infer that both the mouse and the man have changed?	

How do most people feel about mice? Give details about the relationship between humans and mice.

What can you infer about the man's feelings throughout the video? Think about what he *feels* compared with what he *values*.

What lesson does this short teach about caring for others? How could you apply this lesson in your own life?

- ❏ *How do most people feel about mice?* Most people don't want mice inside their homes unless they are pets. Mice are generally considered pests.
- ❏ *How does the man feel about mice?* The man seems to think the mouse is a pest, but he also values its life. We can tell by the way he can't bring himself to harm the mouse, and by how he goes out of his way to care for it.
- ❏ *Lessons from the video*: Being kind to others is important; it is possible to overcome initial bias.

- ❏ Show the short a second time through without stopping. Guide students to answer the three questions at the bottom of the page. These questions are intended to be scaffolded (understanding of the first two is necessary to answer the third). Students may answer the questions in order, or you may choose entry points for students based on readiness.
- ❏ Lead a class discussion: How can visual cues help us to make reasonable inferences? Connect the concept of inferencing to making observations.

Inferencing Lesson 2: Missing Information

Objective: Develop the skill of inferencing in a verbal/textual context.

Materials

- ❏ *This Is Not My Hat* by Jon Klassen (teacher's copy)
- ❏ Handout 3.5: Read Aloud Reflection (one per student)
- ❏ Figure 3.1: Duplicated for each student
- ❏ Handout 3.6: Inferring the Story (one per student)
- ❏ Handout 3.7: Writing the Story (one per student)
- ❏ Handout 3.8: I Have, Who Has? Cards (duplicated front/back and cut apart into individual cards; one set for the whole group)

Whole Group Introduction

- ❏ Remind students that convergent thinkers use inferencing to help them find solutions. Inferencing is the process of using what we *already know combined with the information given* (in a text, visual context, or situation) to fill in gaps and find a solution.

- ❏ Begin with this example scenario: "If you came into our classroom in the morning, and I was not here, but you saw another teacher who you did not know yet sitting at my desk, what could you infer?" (Reasonable answers should be discussed, such as: the teacher is sick, we have a substitute, the teacher is not at school, etc.) Ask students to give reasoning for their thinking, i.e., "We know that [you] are usually at your desk in the morning, but if we didn't know the teacher who was there, we could *infer* that you had a substitute teacher," etc. Point out that it would not be a reasonable inference to guess that, say, "The teacher has been abducted by aliens." This is not something we could support with our schema/observations.
- ❏ Show the anchor chart for inferencing (Handout 3.1). Remind students that we must have solid reasoning to back up an inference, otherwise it is simply a wild guess.

Read Aloud Activity

- ❏ Introduce the book *This Is Not My Hat* by Jon Klassen. This book follows a small fish who has stolen a hat, and a big fish who would like his hat back. Ask students to infer the setting (ocean/sea/pond/lake).
- ❏ As you read the first part of the book, model thinking aloud about inferences. You can infer things like what kind of character the small fish is, why the crab doesn't keep the small fish's secret, and how the big fish feels about his hat being missing. Be sure to include your reasoning to show how you used visual/schema clues to infer.
- ❏ Toward the end of the book, the little fish swims into the plants and can no longer be seen; the big fish follows. The only visual information we get after that is the big fish with his hat back on his head. *Do not* think aloud during this part of the book. Allow students to infer for themselves what has happened. Try to keep students from calling out guesses—they will be able to guess what happened on their Read Aloud Reflection page (Handout 3.5)
- ❏ Distribute the Read Aloud Reflection page (Handout 3.5), allowing students time to complete it and infer what happened in the tall grass, providing their reasoning. See Box 3.3 for key understandings for this read aloud. Allow time to share if possible.

Handout 3.5: Read Aloud Reflection

This is Not My Hat by Jon Klassen

Name: ____

Give a brief summary of the story.	How did the book force the reader to use inferencing?

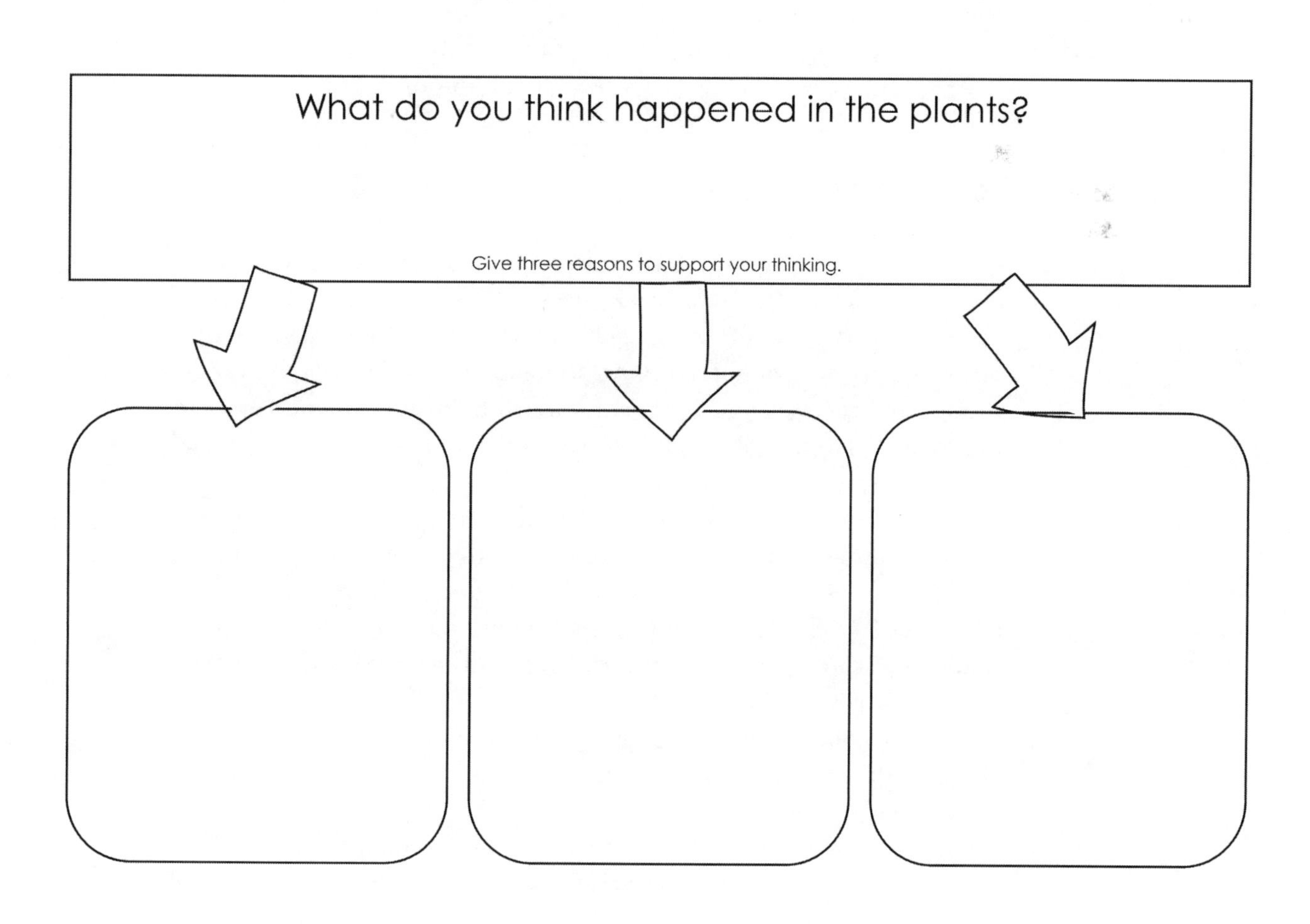

Box 3.3: *This Is Not My Hat* Key Understandings

- ❑ *Story summary*: A small fish has stolen a hat from a big fish. The big fish wants his hat back. The small fish swims into the tall grass to hide from the big fish. When the big fish follows the small fish into the tall grass, we don't get to see what happens, but the final pages of the book show that the big fish has gotten his hat back, and the small fish is nowhere to be found.
- ❑ *Connection to inferencing*: We must infer what happens between the big and small fishes in the tall grass. We aren't able to see what happens, but we can use what happens before and afterward in the story, as well as what we know about food chains, in order to make an inference.
- ❑ *What happened in the tall grass?* While we don't know what actually happens, many students will infer that the bigger fish has eaten the smaller fish in order to retrieve his hat. Others may infer that the small fish gave the hat back willingly.

Skill Development Activity

- ❑ Remind students that inferencing means combining schema with observations to make educated guesses. Distribute the What's the Story? scene (Figure 3.1) to students along with the Inferring the Story recording page (Handout 3.6). Give students time to record their observations and their schema (connections) on this page. Encourage them to add details if they get stuck—we want them to have as much material to work with as possible.
- ❑ Once students have had time to work with the scene and record observations and connections, direct them to cut out both the speech bubble and the thought bubble at the bottom of the recording page (Handout 3.6). Students will fill in a thought and a dialogue on these shapes and then glue them onto the What's the Story? scene (they do not necessarily need to be on the same character!)
- ❑ Finally, distribute the story writing template (Handout 3.7) and give students time to write a paragraph about the What's the Story? scene. Share a few if time allows.
- ❑ Conclude the lesson by playing a round of inferencing "I Have, Who Has?" Duplicate the card pages (Handout 3.8), copying front-to-back, and cut apart the cards. Be sure that you have matching card fronts

Figure 3.1 *Photo of Kids on the Beach* by Ben McLeod on Unsplash.

Handout 3.6: Inferring the Story

Name: ____

Describe the scene. Place yourself in the scene, and think about all of the details you can observe.

Describe your schema. What connections can you make to the scene? Think about things you already know, have done, or have read about.

Cut out the speech and thought bubbles below. Glue them onto the scene, filling in what you can infer might be the thoughts or words of someone in the scene.

Handout 3.7: Writing the Story

Name: ________________________________

Now, write a paragraph telling the story of the scene. Be sure to include what happened before this particular scene as well as what might have happened afterwards! Be creative, and use your observations and schema to make inferences about what might make sense in a story about this scene. Don't forget to include your speech and thought bubbles in the story!

Handout 3.8: I Have, Who Has?

A

Tonight my family will go to Luigi's Italian Restaurant together.

Who Has...

What meal will we eat?

B

I put on my hat, gloves, coat, and scarf before I went to school.

Who Has...

What season is it?

C

We had our suitcases packed and plane tickets in had as we drove down the road.

Who Has...

Where are we going?

D

The guests arrived with gifts which we put on the table. At 4:00 PM, we turned off the lights and hid behind the couch.

Who Has...

What event is happening?

E

My cousin is a baker who loves to try new recipes. When I tasted her latest creation, my mouth puckered!

Who Has...

What kind of flavor was it?

F

It's spring. After recess, his eyes were itching and he kept sneezing.

Who Has...

What's wrong with him?

Handout 3.8, continued: I Have, Who Has?

A **I Have...** TRICK-OR-TREAT	B **I Have...** BREAKFAST
C **I Have...** CAT	D **I Have...** CAMPING
E **I Have...** THE BEACH	F **I Have...** DUCK

Handout 3.8, continued: I Have, Who Has?

G

We went to the water park, got ice cream, and ate dinner outside.

Who Has...

What season is it?

H

We had our tickets ready and wore our favorite player's jersey. We hoped our team would hit a home run!

Who Has...

Where were we going?

I

We were dressed as a witch, a ghost, and a monster as we headed down the street with buckets in hand.

Who Has...

What event is happening?

J

I opened my umbrella as I stepped outside in my rain boots.

Who Has...

What kind of weather are we having?

K

I crawled out of the tent to find Dad making pancakes over the fire pit.

Who Has...

What event is happening?

L

I added a carton of eggs to my basket along with the milk, bread, and lettuce.

Who Has...

Where am I?

Handout 3.8, continued: I Have, Who Has?

G

I Have...

SOUR

H

I Have...

WINTER

I

I Have...

HE HAS ALLERGIES

J

I Have...

AIRPORT

K

I Have...

HE IS SICK

L

I Have...

DINNER

Handout 3.8, continued: I Have, Who Has?

M

He did not go to school today. He stayed in bed, ate soup for lunch, and slept a lot. Mom took his temperature twice.

Who Has...

What is wrong with him?

N

They played all day in the water, built sandcastles, and ate a picnic lunch.

Who Has...

Where are they?

O

I poured my cereal as I watched a morning cartoon.

Who Has...

What meal did I eat?

P

I love my new pet. I can pet her soft fur as she curls up in my lap and purrs.

Who Has...

What pet do I have?

Q

I love to watch my favorite animal at the pond in the park. It's so funny when it waddles up to me and quacks to ask for bread crumbs!

Who Has...

What is my favorite animal?

R

The kids ran as fast as they could. When they finished, Katie got a blue ribbon.

Who Has...

What event is happening?

Handout 3.8, continued: I Have, Who Has?

M **I Have...** A RACE	N **I Have...** GROCERY STORE
O **I Have...** SURPRISE PARTY	P **I Have...** SUMMER
Q **I Have...** BASEBALL GAME	R **I Have...** RAINY

and backs; each card is marked with a letter (A through R) to help make sure that fronts and backs match. In this game, each student will be given a card with a scenario on one side and an inference on the other. (Differentiation: allow students who might need more support to be paired with another student to help). There are 18 cards; some students may have to work in pairs, or some may take more than one card depending on your numbers; all cards should be used.

- ❏ Starting with any student, ask them to read their scenario and "Who Has" question. Students should look at their inferences ("I Have") and see who has an inference that makes the most sense for each scenario. They should provide reasoning for their answers. (For example: "I have *summer.* I know because the clues said that it was hot outside and in summer it's hot.")
- ❏ The student who had that inference will then turn over their card and read their scenario and "Who Has" inferencing question.
- ❏ The game continues in this manner until all cards have been read and inferences have been made.
- ❏ Discuss: What clues did we use to make inferences? Were some cards trickier than others? Why? Reiterate that we needed to use both concrete evidence as well as our existing schema to make accurate inferences.

Inferencing Authentic Application Activity: Shipwreck Scenario

Objective: Apply the skill of inferencing to an authentic problem.

Materials

- ❏ Handout 3.9a and Handout 3.9b: Missing Pieces (differentiated pages duplicated based on student readiness)
- ❏ *The Wretched Stone* by Chris van Allsburg (teacher's copy)
- ❏ Handout 3.10: Shipwreck Survivors Cards
- ❏ Handout 3.11: Belongings Cards

Whole Group Introduction

- ❏ Review the skill of inferencing, displaying the Inferencing Anchor Chart (Handout 3.1). Remind students that we must use both our schema (what we already know) as well as information we learn through a problem to fill in gaps and find solutions.

Handout 3.9a: Missing Pieces 1

Name: ____

Each of the pictures below is missing a part. Can you use your skills of connecting the dots to complete the drawings? Think about what you see, what you know, and what clues you can use from the other parts of the drawing. Cut out the boxes at the bottom and glue them to the picture they complete.

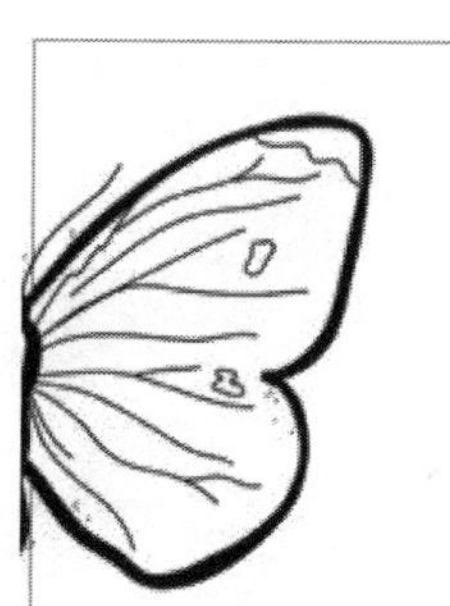

Handout 3.9b: Missing Pieces 2

Name: ____

Each of the pictures below is missing a part. Can you use your skills of connecting the dots to complete the drawings? Think about what you see, what you know, and what clues you can use from the other parts of the drawing.

- ❑ Scaffolding for students' interest and readiness, distribute appropriate levels of the Missing Pieces activity (Handout 3.9a/3.9b). This is presented in two levels, one with more support that may be more appropriate for those who are not inclined to artistic activities (3.9a), and one that is much more abstract, with visual cues removed (3.9b). Choose, or allow students to choose, their complete-the-picture activity based on interest and readiness. In both activities, students will complete pictures that are missing a portion based on what they can already see.
- ❑ Remind students that they should infer what is missing based on what they know combined with what they see.
- ❑ Quickly discuss the activity: How did students use inference to determine what pieces were missing?

Read Aloud Activity

- ❑ Read aloud *The Wretched Stone* by Chris van Allsburg. As you read, think aloud, making and inviting inferences about what is happening. Discuss the book at the conclusion; remind students that they should use schema plus observations to draw inferences about what is happening.
- ❑ This book provides a great bridge to the convergent thinking activity, which centers around a "shipwreck" scenario.

Skill Development Activity

- ❑ In this scenario, there are three options for differentiation. Choose the one that meets your students' readiness/needs. Each is outlined below.
- ❑ Present the shipwreck scenario to the class.

Box 3.4: Shipwreck Scenario

Off the coast of Borneo, several passengers were on a ship that ran aground. The passengers are all fine, but the ship is ruined. Each of the passengers was on their way to a small Pacific Island to do a specific job. Now, all of their belongings that were in the cargo hold are scattered across the beach! Looking around, the investigators need your help. Can you infer whose belongings are whose while the detectives question the passengers about what caused the boat to crash into the shoreline? You'll need to use your convergent thinking skills in inferencing to determine which passengers' things belong together.

Handout 3.10: Shipwreck Survivor Cards

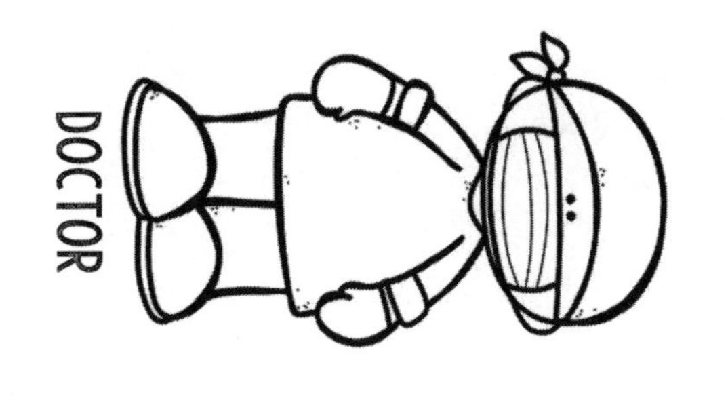

TABLE 3.2
Shipwreck Activity Level 1 Bag Contents

Bag 1: Doctor	Bag 2: Landscape Architect or Builder	Bag 3: Artist
❑ Rubber gloves	❑ Blueprints	❑ Canvases
❑ Face masks	❑ Work boots	❑ Pencil set
❑ First aid kit	❑ Overalls	❑ Folding chair
❑ Computer	❑ Small shovel	❑ Smock
❑ Wet wipes	❑ Set of rulers	❑ Notebook and pens

❑ After you read through the situation, ask students what facts are given. Tell them that their task is to match the belongings with the shipwrecked passengers. Determine challenge level for each small group of students and proceed according to the desired set of directions outlined here.

- **Level 1:** In this level, students will be presented with complete bags of belongings, and asked to determine (infer) what type of person each bag belongs to. They should be able to explain their thinking about why they assigned each bag to each person. Cut apart the Belongings Cards (Handout 3.11) and sort the cards into three separate, unlabeled "bags" (you may either place each set of belongings in a separate envelope/resealable baggie or simply make three separate piles). Suggested bag contents are listed in Table 3.1. Offer students between three and five different "survivor" cards from Handout 3.10 and have them assign the bags to the appropriate survivors based on their inferences about the contents. Note: not all belongings are listed in Table 3.2; use your judgment and add/remove items based on student readiness. Some items are specifically ambiguous (could belong to any of several characters). You can choose to provide the items listed here and then have students add the additional loose items for added challenge as well. For an additional challenge in this activity, you could provide the survivor cards not used here and ask students to create a "bag" of five items that could belong to that person as well!
- **Level 2:** At this level, students will be presented with several loose belongings, and asked to assign each of the loose items to a person with a specified occupation. They must make inferences about why each occupation might need such items on a trip and should also be able to explain their inferences. Cut apart the "belongings" cards (Handout 3.11) and the "survivors" cards (Handout 3.10). Give each

Handout 3.11: Shipwreck Belongings Cards

set of rulers	sun hat	blueprints
wire cutters	rubber gloves	computer
canvases	pencil set	smock
face masks	work boots	wet wipes
first aid kit	overalls	folding chair
small shovel	hammer	notebooks and pens

set to a small group of students and have them assign the belongings to each of the survivors. Then, discuss why each group made the determinations that they did.

- **Level 3:** Students are given several loose belongings and are asked to sort them according to how they infer they would be grouped. They do this without the support of knowing which "people" might have been on the ship; they should infer this based upon the ways they categorize the belongings. Cut apart the "belongings" cards (Handout 3.11). Give each set to a small group of students and have them group the belongings into "suitcases" that make sense to them. Ask them to determine what kind of person each suitcase would belong to. Then, discuss why each group made the determinations that they did.

- ❑ At all levels, students will be asked to infer; the level of support and process are differentiated to require a higher level of abstraction and independence as the levels increase.
- ❑ Discuss with the whole group the process of inferencing. Guide the discussion with questions such as the following:
  - Which items were easier to categorize? Why?
  - What information did we have to use from our background knowledge?
  - Would it have been helpful to have any other information? What?
  - Were there things that might have been in a different category? Explain.

Inferencing Concluding Activities

- ❑ Distribute the Inferencing Exit Ticket (Appendix A). Ask students to reflect on their learning about the skill of using both schema as well as observable facts in order to make inferences. Allow time for students to complete the exit ticket. Use this as a formative assessment, to gain a better understanding of your students' readiness to effectively practice the skill.
- ❑ If desired, complete the Group Inferencing Rubric (Appendix A) to track students' progress with the skill.
- ❑ If desired, use the Convergent Thinking Student Observation Rubric (Appendix A) to assess and quantify individual students' mastery.
- ❑ Ask students to retrieve their Convergent Thinking Avatar (Handout I.3). In the Inferencing box, they should either write the main ideas of this section or illustrate their avatar using the skill of inferencing.

Bibliography

Haniyya P.M. (August 13, 2020). The box/la boîte. By ESMA. https://www.youtube.com/watch?v=QN5lvmmqIM8.

Klassen, J. (2012). *This is not my hat.* Somerville, MA: Candlewick Press.

Photo of kids on the beach by Ben McLeod on unsplash. (n.d.). https://unsplash.com/@ben_mcleod

Tallec, O. (2016). *Who, what, where?* San Francisco, CA: Chronicle Books.

Van Allsburg, C. (1991). *The wretched stone.* Boston, MA: Houghton Mifflin.

CHAPTER 4

Sub-Skill 4

Deduction

TABLE 4.1
Deduction Sub-Skill Overview

Thinking Skill Outline	
Focus Questions	❑ How can we use our observations and schema to make predictions? ❑ What information is missing? Can we make a guess to fill some of the gaps?
Lesson 1	*Using Clues to Confirm* ❑ **Trade Book Focus:** *Under the Lemon Moon* by Edith Hope Fine ❑ **Practice Activity:** Pairing and Ordering: Students will work with clues to deduce correct pairs, orders, and arrangements in a series of logic puzzles.
Lesson 2	*Using Clues to Eliminate* ❑ **Trade Book Focus:** *Deductive Detective* by Brian Rock ❑ **Practice Activity:** Deductive Logic Grids: Students will use clues to eliminate possibilities and narrow to a single solution within deductive logic grid puzzles.
Authentic Application Activity	*Get a Clue!* ❑ **Practice Activity:** Students will read a story problem and use clues from various sources and puzzles, piecing together information to arrive at a solution.

DOI: 10.4324/9781003268307-5

Deduction Lesson 1: Using Clues to Confirm

Objective: Develop the concept of using deduction to confirm ideas and create order.

Materials

- ❏ Handout 4.2: Logical Picture Pairs (one for display)
- ❏ *Under the Lemon Moon* by Edith Hope Fine (teacher's copy)
- ❏ Handout 4.3: Read Aloud Reflection
- ❏ Handout 4.4: Logical Pairs (duplicated as needed)
- ❏ Handout 4.5: Logical Orders 1 (duplicated as needed)
- ❏ Handout 4.6: Logical Orders 2 (duplicated as needed)
- ❏ Handout 4.7: Logical Orders 3 (duplicated as needed)

Whole Group Introduction

- ❏ Introduce the concept of deduction. Tell students that deduction is a process of gathering clues in order to confirm or eliminate possible solutions. Display the Deduction Anchor Chart (Handout 4.1). Discuss the image on the poster—each clue goes into a funnel and comes together to confirm a single solution. The skill of deduction is like the funnel; we must take all the ideas and clues into consideration, but in the end, these clues will be combined to reveal a single solution.
- ❏ Either project or display Handout 4.2 (Logical Picture Pairs). Ask students to think about how we could logically pair the various characters' items (Cinderella with a lost shoe, the baker with the oven, the pirate with the treasure map, the astronaut with the rocket). Discuss the following questions: What clues helped us to make matches? What clues and schema helped us eliminate possibilities? Using the clues we have available, including observation and inferencing, we are able to find solutions that make sense.

Handout 4.1: Deduction Anchor Chart

DEDUCTION

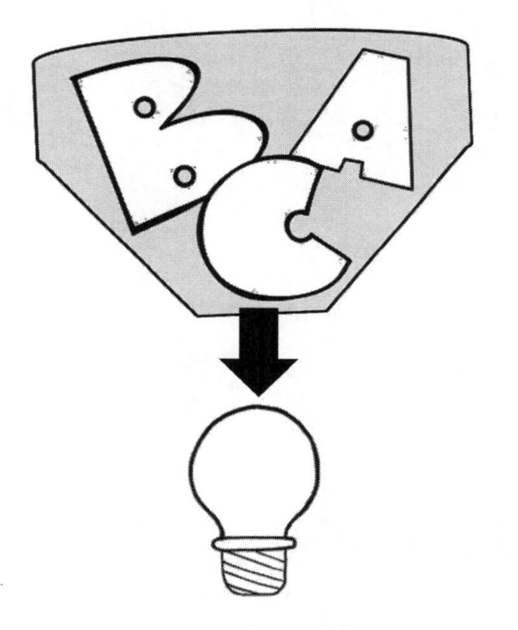

USING CLUES TO CONFIRM SOLUTIONS

Handout 4.2: Logical Picture Pairs

Read Aloud Activity

- ❑ Tell students that today you'll be reading aloud a book called *Under the Lemon Moon*. In this story, Rosalinda experiences something and must use deduction to help her find a solution that will bring healing to both herself and her lemon tree.
- ❑ Read aloud, stopping to think aloud about the clues Rosalinda finds (clues about how to help her tree as well as clues about the "Night Man.") Point out her deductive thinking processes (each of the proposed solutions for the tree are eliminated as she has already tried them; she confirms the Night Man's situation and develops a solution that will help everyone and bring joy).
- ❑ Help students to complete the Read Aloud Reflection page (Handout 4.3). Discuss student responses, relating back to the skill of deduction. For key understandings, see Box 4.1.

Box 4.1: *Under the Lemon Moon* Key Understandings

- ❑ *Story summary*: Late one night, Rosalinda sees someone stealing all the lemons off of her beloved prize lemon tree. In the morning, her tree is damaged and seems to be dying. She seeks out help for her tree from friends and family, eventually finding the Night Man who stole her lemons. In healing her tree, she is able to bestow a kindness on the man, who she finds may have needed her lemons more than she did herself.
- ❑ *Connection to deduction*: Rosalinda receives all sorts of advice about how to help her tree. She must think through what she has already tried and what she has not in order to find a solution that heals both her tree and her hurt feelings.
- ❑ *Details about the Night Man*: He is a thief. When we find him later in the story, we see him selling Rosalinda's lemons in the marketplace. His wife is with him, and his children are behind him playing with stones. They wear shabby clothing.
- ❑ *What we can deduce about the Night Man*: He had a need for the lemons in order to earn money to feed his family. They are very poor.
- ❑ *What we can infer about Rosalinda*: She is a generous person who cares about others.

Handout 4.3: Read Aloud Reflection

Under the Lemon Moon by Edith Hope Fine

Name: ____

Summarize the main idea of the story.

How did the book use deduction?

Give as many details as possible about the Night Man. Be sure to include his actions and your observations!

What can we deduce about the reason the Night Man stole the lemons?

BONUS: What can you INFER about Rosalinda based on her treatment of the Night Man?

Skill Development Activity

- ❑ Distribute the Logical Pairs and Logical Orders practice pages (Handouts 4.4, 4.5, 4.6, and 4.7) to students. Use as desired; students do not necessarily need to do all of them, although they may. You may choose to use these activities in any order/combination that works for your students. See Box 4.2 for solutions to Handouts 4.6 and 4.7.
- ❑ Working in pairs or independently, allow students to complete these practice pages, using deduction to confirm their solutions and create order within each puzzle.
- ❑ As students work, circulate and monitor understanding of the deduction process. Look for students to begin to become more efficient in their use of clues, seeing orders, patterns, and pairs more intuitively as they practice.
- ❑ Conclude the lesson by bringing the whole group back together for a debriefing session. Ask formative assessment questions, such as the following:
  - What clues caused you to place things in this order?
  - Do any clues point to a different order/pair?
  - What helps you be sure that you have the correct order/pair?
  - How do these activities help us better understand deduction?

Box 4.2: Solutions for Handouts 4.6 and 4.7

Handout 4.6: The paragraph should read as follows:
We went to the park to play on the playground. I ran to the swings, my favorite part of the playground. A cloud started to form, covering the bright sunshine. I thought I felt a raindrop, but I was having so much fun I ignored it. All of a sudden, it started pouring down rain. We ran as fast as we could to the car, but we still got soaked.
Handout 4.7: The sentences should read as follows:

- ❑ What do you think we should do?
- ❑ The boys went to the store.
- ❑ My snowman has melted away.
- ❑ The sun is shining in the sky.

Handout 4.4: Logical Pairs

Name: ____________________

Cut apart the verbs and adverbs at the bottom of the page. Use your deductive logic to pair them. Then, use the pairs to create eight unique sentences, one using each of your logical pairs.

1	
2	
3	
4	
5	
6	
7	
8	

VERBS

cry	sleep
laugh	talk
walk	write
dance	eat

ADVERBS

quietly	*firmly*
loudly	*quickly*
peacefully	*neatly*
wildly	*freely*

Handout 4.5: Logical Orders 1

Name: ____

Cut apart the pictures below. Glue them on a separate page in the most logical order. Then, write the story of what happens in the pictures on the lines below.

____

____

____

____

____

____

____

Handout 4.6: Logical Orders 2

Name: ______________________________

Cut apart the sentences at the bottom of the page and rearrange them to form a story in a logical order. Glue the story strips between the boxes below. Then, add a part to the story telling what happens both before and afterwards. Be sure to use deduction to think about what makes the most sense!

Glue sentence strips here in the most logical order.

A cloud started to form, covering the bright sunshine.

All of a sudden, it started pouring down rain.

We went to the park to play on the playground.

We ran as fast as we could to the car, but we still got soaked.

I thought I felt a raindrop, but I was having so much fun I ignored it.

I ran to the swings, my favorite part of the playground.

Handout 4.7: Logical Orders 3

Name: ___________________________________

The sentences below are all mixed up. Can you use logic and deduction to rearrange the words and put them into sentences that make sense?

DO YOU SHOULD WE DO WHAT THINK	
STORE TO WENT BOYS THE THE	
AWAY SNOWMAN MELTED HAS MY	
SKY SHINING SUN THE THE IN IS	
QUICKLY MY ATE I SUPPER	
WEEKEND ARE PLANS YOUR WHAT FOR THE	
DELICIOUS FRUIT WAS JUICY THE AND	
I HAD READ COULD I MY BOOK THE FIND BEFORE TO	
MATH LOVE LEARN SCHOOL AT WE TO	
TO GO PLAY NEED I SNOW COAT WEAR A TO IN THE	

- ❑ I quickly ate my supper *or* Quickly, I ate my supper.
- ❑ What are your plans for the weekend?
- ❑ The fruit was delicious and juicy *or* juicy and delicious.
- ❑ I had to find my book before I could read *or* Before I could read, I had to find my book.
- ❑ At school, we love to learn math *or* We love to learn math at school.
- ❑ I need to wear a coat to go play in the snow *or* To go play in the snow, I need to wear a coat.

Deduction Lesson 2: Using Clues to Eliminate

Objective: Develop the skill of using deductive reasoning to eliminate possibilities, finding solutions by process of elimination.

Materials

- ❑ *Deductive Detective* by Brian Rock (teacher's copy)
- ❑ Handout 4.8: Deductive Detective Character Cards (one per student)
- ❑ Handout 4.9a/b: Read Aloud Reflection (copied front-to-back; one per student)
- ❑ Handout 4.10: Logic Puzzles Level 1 (duplicate as needed)
- ❑ Handout 4.11: Logic Puzzles Level 2 (duplicate as needed)
- ❑ Handout 4.12: Logic Puzzles Level 3 (duplicate as needed)
- ❑ Handout 4.13a/b: Logic Puzzle Extension (duplicate as needed)

Whole Group Introduction

- ❑ Remind students that deduction involves using what we know to confirm or eliminate possible solutions.
- ❑ Model deduction by asking: "If we know that *only* people with blue eyes like soup, who do we know *doesn't* like soup? If it snows tonight, and I see pawprints in my yard in the morning, is it reasonable to deduce that they were not made by a giraffe? What animals does that eliminate? Which does it not?"

- ❏ Tell students that they will need to use good deductive reasoning; we need to use what we see, what we know, and what we can confirm with facts. We must have reasoning to back up our conclusions.

Read Aloud Activity

- ❏ Prepare for the read aloud by making one copy of the character cards (Handout 4.8) for each student. Students will also need to have the Read Aloud Reflection page (Handout 4.9a/4.9b), copied front-to-back (flip along the long side) to create a page with pockets.
- ❏ Distribute character cards to students. Ask them to cut apart the 12 characters and have them out and ready as you read the story aloud.
- ❏ Read aloud *Deductive Detective.* Stop at each page, allowing students to find the character who was eliminated on each page. On the front of the character card next to the animal's picture, students should place a number indicating the order in which the animals are eliminated. On the reverse, students should make a note of what eliminated each character (and importantly, consider if it was an *action* or a *trait* which caused that character to be eliminated).
- ❏ Following the read aloud, distribute the Read Aloud Reflection page (Handout 4.9a/4.9b). Ask students to write a six-word summary of the story, and a few words about how the story used deduction at the top. Then, guide students through the process of cutting and folding up the bottom of their paper to form two pockets, following the directions at the bottom of the page.
  - ■ To do this, students will look at the bottom of their page, following the directions to cut along the dotted line and fold up the two flaps. They will tape each flap vertically, creating two "pockets" in which they can place their character cards from Handout 4.8.
- ❏ Guide students through sorting the characters into their respective pockets. Then, discuss the generalization question, and help students write a generalization about using the skill of deduction. Look for students to include some or all of the objective skills: *Deduction is the process of using information to confirm or eliminate suspicions and find a solution.* Key understandings for this Read Aloud Reflection are outlined in Box 4.3.

Handout 4.8: Deductive Detective Character Cards

Handout 4.9a: Read Aloud Reflection

Deductive Detective by Brian Rock

Name: ______________________________

Summarize the main idea of the story.	How did the book use deduction?

Fold here

Fold here

Cut your paper along the vertical line. Fold up one half to the horizontal line, and tape along both edges to make a pocket. Then do the same for the other half so that you have two pockets.

Handout 4.9b: Read Aloud Reflection (reverse)

Deductive Detective by Brian Rock

In this pocket, place the animal cards who were eliminated as suspects by **because of physical evidence. (TRAITS)**

In this pocket, place the animal cards who were eliminated as suspects by **because of something they did or did not do. (ACTIONS)**

Write a generalization about the process of deduction that includes ways you can eliminate or confirm suspicions and gives a tip for success.

Box 4.3: *Deductive Detective* Key Understandings

- ❑ *Story summary*: In this story, a cake is missing. Twelve animal suspects are considered and eliminated, one by one, until the culprit is revealed.
- ❑ *Connection to deduction*: Each suspect is eliminated based upon the available clues until we are left with a single solution—the culprit!
- ❑ *Characters who are eliminated due to traits*: Kangaroo (size), mouse (size), elephant (size), moose (antlers), swan (feathers), pig (tail), tiger (paws).
- ❑ *Characters who are eliminated due to actions*: Horse (won't go in a dark room), rooster (crowing at dawn), raccoon (climbs trees, doesn't swing from them), cow (doesn't jump).
- ❑ *Generalizations*: Potential solutions can be eliminated for a variety of reasons, so good detectives should use all the clues available to deduce solutions.

Skill Development Activity

- ❑ Tell students that they will be working with their deductive logic skills to solve some clue-based puzzles. Logic Puzzles, often called elimination grids, require students to use clues to deduce the answers. The puzzles grow in complexity as the unit progresses, beginning with a simple grid explained below. Often, students must read all the way through the clues first and then go back to the top to begin deducing the answer.
- ❑ Guide students through solving a logic elimination grid problem as a whole group.
  - ■ Present students with a logic problem scenario: Marty Mouse went to stay with his cousin, Mortimer, for the weekend. As a way of thanking Mortimer for a wonderful visit, Marty sent his cousin a gift on three different days the following week. Using logic and deduction, we will figure out which day Mortimer received each treat.
  - ■ Guide students to glean important information from the problem: three treats were sent, each on a different day. Remind students that Mortimer would only have received one treat each day, so we need to match the days with the treats.

- ■ Draw a 4 × 4 grid on the board. Tell students that in order to organize our information and clues, we can use a **logic elimination grid** to help us solve the problem.
- ■ Label columns 2, 3, and 4 *Tuesday, Wednesday,* and *Thursday.* Label rows 2, 3, and 4 *cheese, hat,* and *bread.*

❑ Now, tell students that we have some clues to help us solve the puzzle. Read aloud clue number 1: **The cheese was received after the hat**. To keep up with this information, we will eliminate any possibilities that cannot be true based on our clue. Therefore, we should mark an X (elimination mark) in the Tuesday column/cheese row because the cheese can't come first (see Table 4.2).

Ensure students understand the process of marking eliminated possibilities in the grid. Then, read aloud clue number 2: **The non-food item was received second**. Students should recognize that the hat is the only non-food item and should realize quickly that the second day in this case is on Wednesday. The student should then mark an O (confirmation mark) in the Wednesday/hat box (column 3, row 3). Draw students' attention to the fact that if the hat was given on Wednesday, then we know the hat wasn't given on Tuesday or Thursday (it could only be given on a single day), so Xs are placed in the corresponding boxes to show that these possibilities are eliminated. We also know the cheese and bread weren't received on Wednesday, so we can eliminate these possibilities as well by marking Xs in the corresponding boxes (see Table 4.3).

Now, using the process of deductive elimination, we can see the cheese must have been given on Thursday and the bread must have been given on Tuesday, as these are the only possibilities left. (See Table 4.4)

TABLE 4.2
Model Logic Elimination Grid after Clue 1

	Tuesday	Wednesday	Thursday
cheese	X		
hat			
bread			

TABLE 4.3
Model Logic Elimination Grid after Clue 2

	Tuesday	Wednesday	Thursday
cheese	X	X	
hat	X	O	X
bread		X	

TABLE 4.4
Completed Model Logic Elimination Grid

	Tuesday	Wednesday	Thursday
cheese	X	X	O
hat	X	O	X
bread	O	X	X

- ❑ Now, students will work to complete some logic elimination grid problems, either on their own, with peer group support (partners/small groups), or with teacher support. There are three leveled logic elimination grid puzzles included here. You may use these to scaffold as needed. Two approaches to differentiate this activity for appropriate student support are:
  - ■ "I do, we do, you do": In this approach, you would model the problem-solving with the Level 1 problem, ask students to work through the Level 2 problem with a partner and teacher support, and then ask them to work through the Level 3 problem independently.
  - ■ Tiered Entry: In this approach, you could assign problems based upon student readiness and ability.
- ❑ If students are ready for an additional challenge, they may choose to tackle the extension problem: The Wedding Party (Handout 4.13a/4.13b). This is a complex problem, but students who enjoy these types of puzzles and are ready for a more extended challenge may have this option.

Box 4.4: Logic Puzzle Answer Keys

- ❑ Level 1: The beetle was caught at 4:00; the fly was caught at 2:00; the gnat was caught at 1:00; and the ladybug was caught at 3:00.
- ❑ Level 2: Milo had the green bed and enjoyed chasing mice; Max had the red bed and enjoyed clawing; Mia had the blue bed and enjoyed sleeping.
- ❑ Level 3: Laura liked sushi and lemonade and had a cat; Liam liked soup and juice and had a dog; Lindsay liked hamburgers and milk and had a bird; Leo liked pizza and tea and had a fish; Lisa liked tacos and water and had a hamster.
- ❑ Extension Challenge:

- ❑ Conclude the lesson by asking students to verbalize a one-sentence takeaway: How did deduction help us solve problems?

Handout 4.10: Deductive Logic Puzzle 1

Name: ______________________________

Level 1

The Spider's Webs

A spider spent all day weaving a web to catch her supper. By nightfall, the spider was delighted to have caught so many insects in her web. Each insect landed on her web at a different time. See if you can figure out when each insect landed in her web.

1. The black and red insect was caught second to last.
2. By the time the beetle landed on the spider's web she was full.
3. The smallest insect was caught first.

	1:00	**2:00**	**3:00**	**4:00**
beetle				
fly				
gnat				
ladybug				

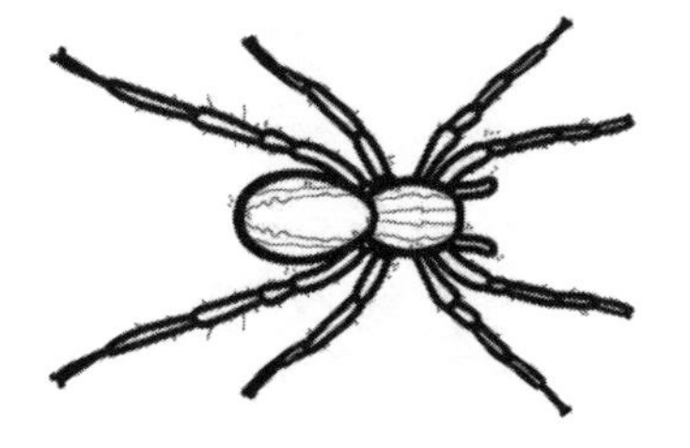

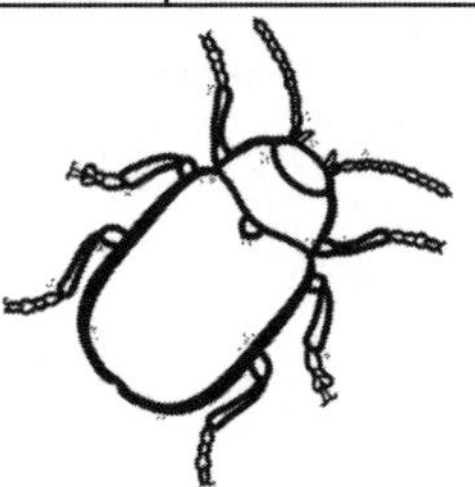

Handout 4.11: Deductive Logic Puzzle 2

Name: ______________________________

Level 2

The Cat's Meow

Three cats named Milo, Max, and Mia each lived with a girl named Sally. Sally gave each cat a different colored cat bed, and each cat had a different favorite activity. Use the clues, match the cats to their bed colors and favorite activities.

1. The cat who liked clawing had neither the green nor the blue bed.
2. Milo's bed was not blue.
3. Mia left the clawing and the mouse-chasing to the boys.
4. Max never practiced with his claws on his lovely red bed.

	Red	Blue	Green	Clawing	Chasing Mice	Sleeping
Milo						
Max						
Mia						

Handout 4.12: Deductive Logic Puzzle 3

Name: ____

Level 3

The Long Siblings

The five Long siblings each have names that start with the letter 'L': Liam, Lisa, Leo, Lindsay, and Laura. Each has a different favorite food and drink, and each has their own pet to take care of. Use the clues to match the children with their favorite food and drink as well as their pets.

1. Leo would not be caught dead eating raw fish.
2. Neither Lisa nor Liam liked pizza, and neither had a cat.
3. Leo loved to watch his fish swimming around the tank, but he did not like either tacos or lemonade.
4. The sibling whose favorites were milk and hamburgers also had a pet bird.
5. The sibling who loved juice also had a dog named Fido.
6. Leo, Lindsay, and the cat-owner did not like tacos or juice.
7. Lisa loved tacos but did not drink milk; Liam loved all kinds of soup, but preferred other drinks over water.

?	pizza	hamburgers	tacos	sushi	soup	lemonade	milk	juice	water	tea	hamster	fish	bird	dog	cat
Laura															
Liam															
Lindsay															
Leo															
Lisa															

Handout 4.13a: Deductive Logic Puzzle Extension

Name: ______________________________

The Flower Loft hosted a wedding last night, and as the staff was cleaning, they found a diamond tennis bracelet on one of the chairs. They need to piece back together the seating arrangement from the party so that they can return the valuable piece of jewelry to its rightful owner. Can you help them? Use the clues and the room layout map to help you.

1. Each couple sat at a table together.
2. At the Iris Table, Travis Ross, Tom Walker, and Robert Pike sat next to their wives, but not next to each other.
3. The Rose table hosted all the single guests. Ben and Gary were excited to catch up with each other, so they sat across from each other. Both William and Violet were running late, so they ended up with the seats closest to the door.
4. Anna and John Smith sat at the heads of one table, where they introduced their friends Susan Wilson and Chris Roberts to Bill and Olivia Marsh.
5. Seated at the Lily Table were two families: the Scotts and the Myers. The children, Sarah and Josh, sat at the heads of the table.
6. Lily Pike was not seated at the Lily Table but was next to her husband. Ava, Violet, and Julia all came by themselves.
7. Emily was across from Carey, who was directly behind Gary. Ella and David Myer were excited to sit right behind their friends the Marshes.
8. Sarah Scott sat between her mother, Millie, and Mrs. Myer.
9. Guests who sat at the heads of the tables were: Lily, Ava, Anna, Sarah, Josh, John, Tom, and William.
10. At both the Tulip and Lily Tables, the women sat on one end and the men on the other. At the Rose and Iris Tables, the seating pattern was alternated (boy/girl).

If the bracelet was found on the seat of the chair at the head of the Tulip Table, who does it belong to?

Handout 4.13b: Deductive Logic Puzzle Extension

Name: ____

DOOR

LILY

ROSE

TULIP

IRIS

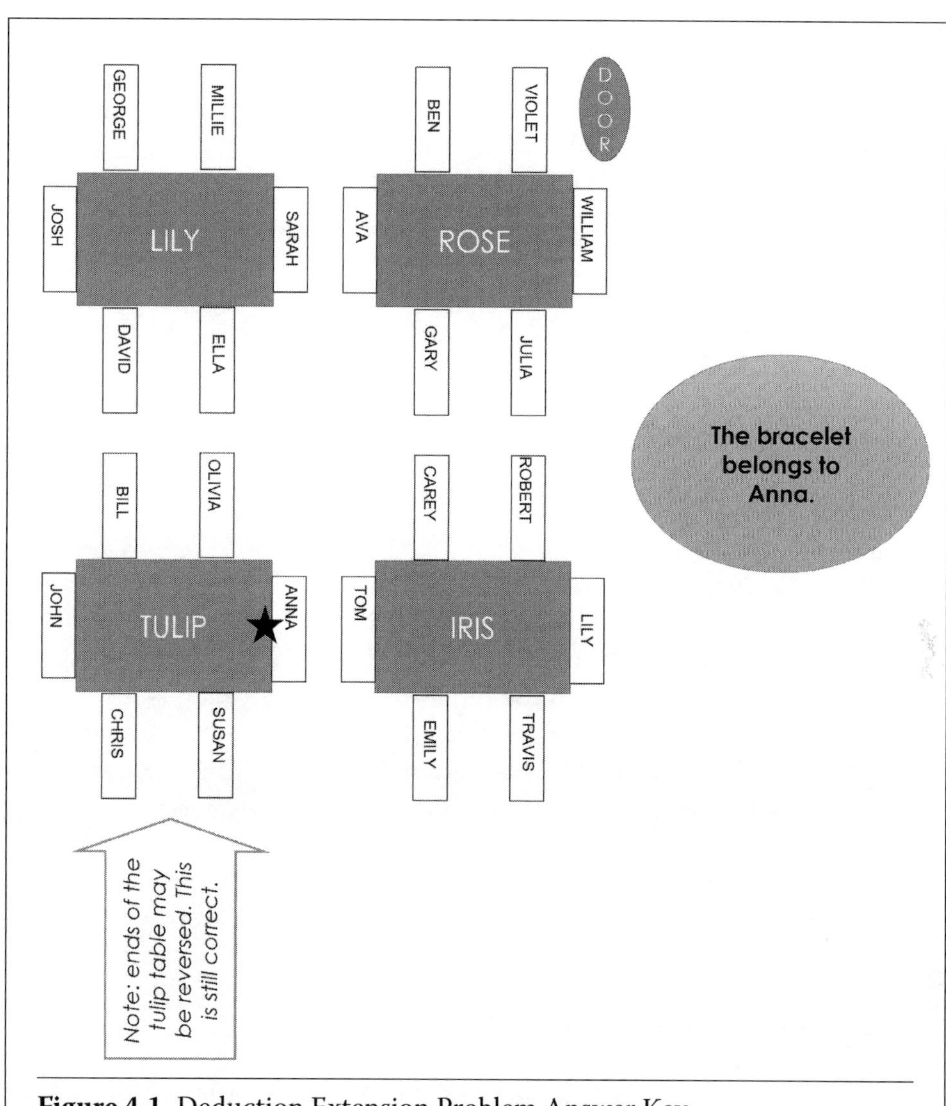

Figure 4.1 Deduction Extension Problem Answer Key

Deduction Authentic Application Activity: Get a Clue!

Objective: Apply the skill of deduction to an authentic problem.

Materials

- ❑ Handout 4.14: Get a Clue! Mini-Booklet

Whole Group Introduction

- ❑ Review with students the thinking skill: Deduction. Emphasize that this skill combines all the other deductive thinking skills they have learned up to this point. They will need to observe, infer, use deduction, and reflect on the information they gather. Then, they will need to organize this information in order to arrive at a solution.
- ❑ Have students turn and talk to review each convergent thinking skill they have learned thus far (observation, inferencing, gathering evidence, deduction). They will use them all for this activity.

Skill Development Activity

- ❑ Prepare the Get a Clue! story booklet (Handout 4.14) for each student.
  - ■ Fold the front/back cover in half. The crease should be on the left side of the front cover.
  - ■ Fold each of the inner pages in half with the text facing outward. The crease should be on the right side of the even-numbered pages.
  - ■ Stack folded book pages so that even page numbers are stacked sequentially facing the top, starting with page 2.
  - ■ Place the stack of folded interior pages inside of the folded cover page. Loose edges should be against the cover's fold, with the creased edge of the internal pages facing outward.
  - ■ Staple along the left-hand side, using the provided staple lines as a guide.
  - ■ If desired, place a strip of tape along the left-hand side to cover the staples, trimming any excess.
- ❑ Grouping students to scaffold support as needed, allow students to work as independently as possible through the booklet. They will need to problem-solve on each page of the booklet, filling in answers as they go.

Handout 4.14: Get a Clue! Mini-Booklet

Name: ______________________________

Using Deduction to Solve

SUPPORT MATERIAL

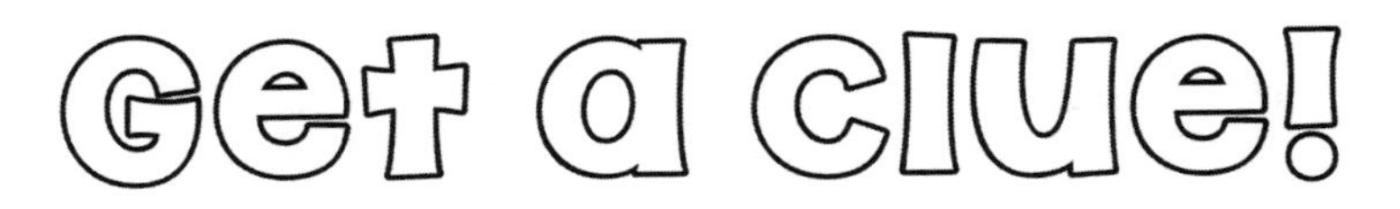

It's a beautiful April day. You are just arriving home when your mom tells you that you got a letter in the mail.

You race to open it, and when you do, you are immediately confused. This isn't a message you can read! It's all in some sort of code. You'll have to work to think like a detective.

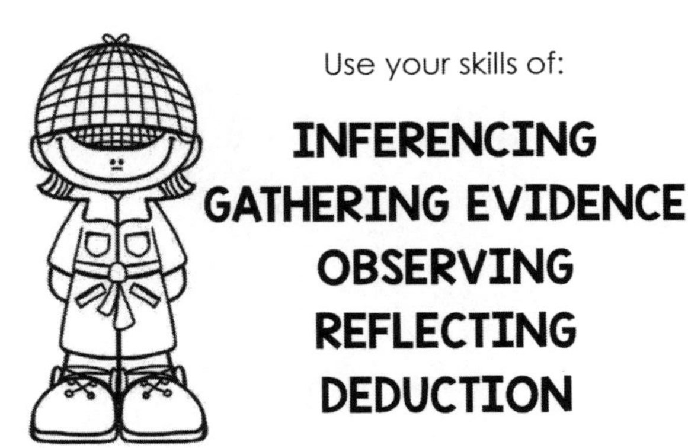

Use your skills of:

INFERENCING
GATHERING EVIDENCE
OBSERVING
REFLECTING
DEDUCTION

...to decode the message and see if you can figure out who sent it—and why!

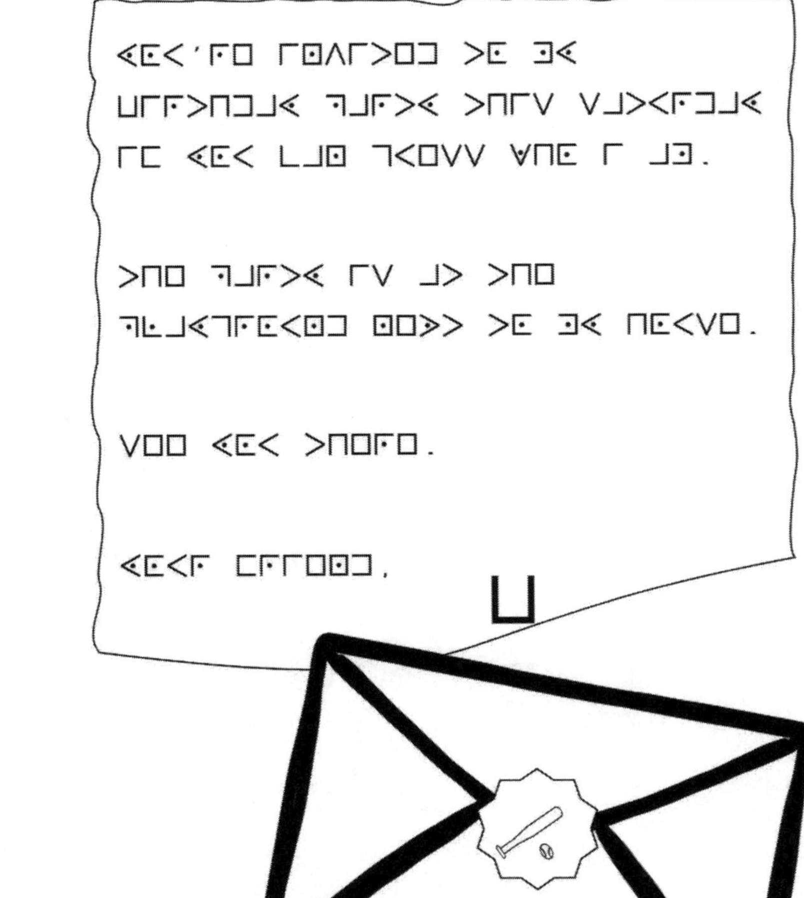

First things first, you have to investigate the letter. Something tells you that you've seen this kind of code before, and then it hits you—it's a Pig-Pen Cipher!

The Pigpen Cipher is a simple geometrical substitution cipher, which exchanges letters for symbols which a pieces of a grid. The key below shows the most commonly used Pigpen Cipher.

The Pigpen Cipher was created by the Freemasons so they could keep documents safe. It was also used by the confederate soldiers during the Civil War. It was named The Pigpen Cipher because the box's look like pigpens and the dots look like pigs. It seems complicated but it isn't really. The lines surrounding the letter and the dots within those lines are the symbols.

A	B	C
D	E	F
G	H	I

J	K	L
M	N	O
P	Q	R

S T U V

W X Y Z

What clues can you learn from the letter?

The letter revealed that the birthday party's location is at:

______________________________,

so

you need to figure out who lives close to there. Look at the map and use these clues about where your friends live to help you.

1. Bella and Beau can walk to the grocery store, but not to school.
2. Briana, Bennett, Brandon, Benjamin, and Bailey all live south of school but north of the hospital.
3. Bailey loves that she has a neighbor to play with across Love Circle.
4. Briana and Bennett are next-door neighbors, and they walk together across Dogwood Court to school each morning.
5. Benjamin's mom picks up Brandon for carpool on the way to school each morning, since Brandon lives on Oak Avenue, and it's on their way.

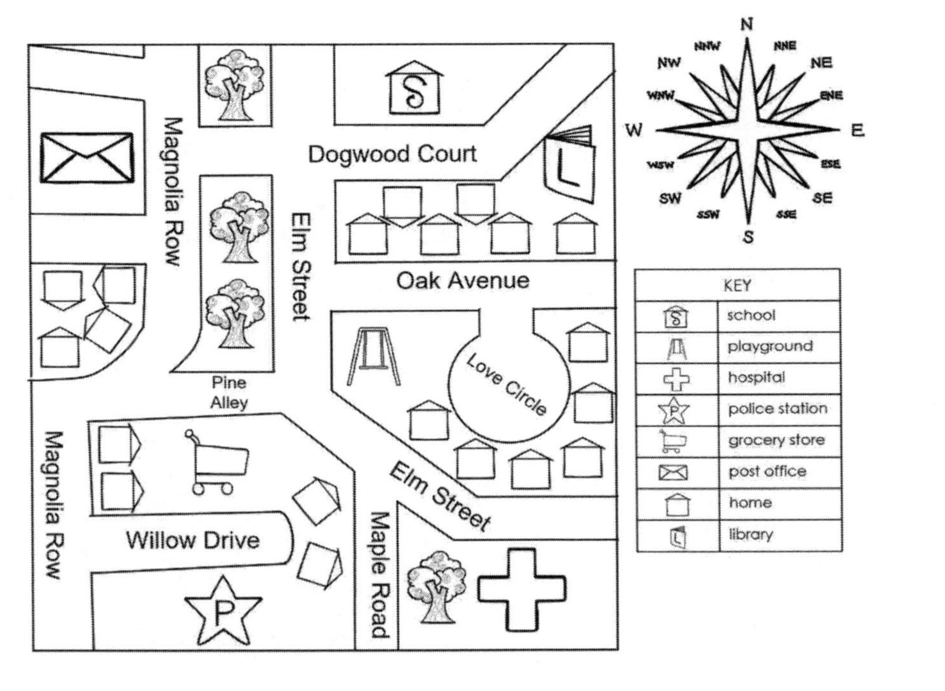

What clues can you learn from the map?

SUPPORT MATERIAL

You feel stuck—these clues can be confusing, and you don't have a clear answer yet! As you sit and wonder, you take one more glance at the envelope the invitation came in. Suddenly, you notice something you don't remember seeing before!

It's

______________________________________!

That sticker on the envelope must be a clue. You decide to think through which one of your friends would have been most likely to put that sticker there.

Use these reflections to help you solve the logic elimination grid and decide who might have sent that invitation.

1. All your friends play a sport. Brandon, Bella, and Bridget's sports don't require any running.
2. Only the sports played by Benjamin, Bailey, Bennett, and Briana require a ball.
3. Both Bella and Beau are part of the relay team in their sports.
4. Both Brandon and Briana try to score goals in their sports, but Brandon scores his on the ice and Briana on a field.
5. Bennett's sport doesn't require any special equipment, but Benjamin needs a bat and Bailey needs a racquet.

	Baseball	Hockey	Basketball	Swimming	Tennis	Track	Cycling	Soccer
Brandon								
Bailey								
Benjamin								
Bella								
Bennett								
Briana								
Beau								
Bridget								

What clues can you learn from this puzzle?

Great work! Now, you recall that the letter also said that the party is this upcoming Saturday, so we need to figure out who has a birthday this month!

As you consider, you remember the following facts about your friends' birthdays. Use them to help you solve the logic elimination grid and determine whose party might be coming up!

1. Bailey celebrates her birthday in a month with an Irish holiday.
2. Bennett and Bridget have birthdays in the same month, but they are the only two friends who have birthdays in that month.
3. Brandon's birthday is one week before Bailey's.

	March	March	April	April	April	April	May	May
Brandon								
Bailey								
Benjamin								
Bella								
Bennett								
Briana								
Beau								
Bridget								

What clues can you learn from this puzzle?

SUPPORT MATERIAL

Now that you've **gathered a lot of evidence** through **observation, deduction,** and **inferencing**, it's time to **reflect** on what you've learned so that you can connect the dots and figure out who sent the invitation! Use the table below to help you organize your evidence.

	Birthday in April?	Lives near playground?	Loves baseball?	Sent the invitation?
Brandon				
Bailey				
Benjamin				
Bella				
Bennett				
Briana				
Beau				
Bridget				

Have you arrived at a solution? What is it?

SUPPORT MATERIAL

Write a summary of how you solved this mystery. Be sure to include how you used your thinking skills of **inferencing, gathering evidence, observation, deduction, and reflection.**

- ❑ On the last page of the booklet, they will complete a reflection, writing step-by-step how they used convergent thinking skills to solve the problem.
- ❑ Discuss and reflect as a whole group. Monitor students for understanding and give small hints and redirections if they seem to be getting off course. Look for students who are attuned to details (observations), solve the problems and puzzles efficiently (inferring and deducting), and are able to put the pieces together in the end to come up with a solution (reflection/connecting the dots).
- ❑ See Box 4.5 for Get a Clue! Answer Key.

Box 4.5: Get a Clue! Answer Key

- ❑ **p. 3–4:** The message reads: You're invited to my birthday party this Saturday if you can guess who I am. The party is at the playground next to my house. See you there. Your friend, B.
- ❑ **p. 5–6:** The party is being held at *the playground.* The clues indicate that only Benjamin, Bailey, and Brandon live "next to" the playground as the invitation states.
- ❑ **p. 7–8:** On the envelope is *a baseball sticker.* The sports each child plays are as follows: Brandon—hockey; Bailey—tennis; Benjamin—*baseball*; Bella—swimming; Bennett—basketball; Briana—soccer; Beau—track; Bridget—cycling.
- ❑ **p. 9:** Brandon and Bailey have birthdays in March; Bennett and Bridget have birthdays in May; Benjamin, Bella, Briana, and Beau have birthdays in April. Since page 1 says "It was a beautiful *April* day..." the party must be for either Benjamin, Bella, Briana, or Beau.
- ❑ **p. 10:** By placing checkmarks in the columns where appropriate, the students should find that only *Benjamin* meets all the criteria, and he was the sender of the invitation.

Deduction Concluding Activities

- ❑ Distribute the Deduction Exit Ticket (Appendix A). Ask students to reflect on their learning about the skill using deduction to both confirm and eliminate possible solutions. Allow time for students to complete the exit ticket. Use this as a formative assessment, to gain a better understanding of your students' readiness to effectively practice the skill.

- ❑ If desired, complete the Group Deduction Rubric (Appendix A) to track students' progress with the skill.
- ❑ If desired, use the Convergent Thinking Student Observation Rubric (Appendix A) to assess and quantify individual students' mastery.
- ❑ Ask students to retrieve their Convergent Thinking Avatar (Handout I.3). In the Deduction box, they should either record the main ideas about the thinking skill or illustrate their avatar using the skill of deduction.

Bibliography

Fine, E.H. (2010). *Under the lemon moon*. New York: National Geographic School Publishing.

Rock, B. (2013). *Deductive detective*. Mt Pleasant, SC: Sylvan Dell Publishing.

CHAPTER 5

Sub-Skill 5

Reflection

TABLE 5.1
Reflection Sub-Skill Overview

Thinking Skill Outline	
Focus Questions	❏ How can we avoid jumping to conclusions? ❏ How does thinking back on choices and experiences help us to gain deeper understanding?
Lesson 1	*Reflecting on Experiences* ❏ **Trade Book Focus:** *Millie Fierce* by Jane K. Manning ❏ **Practice Activity:** "Bridge": Students will watch a short clip to see how reflecting on observations of behavior informs future choices, and then participate in a bridge game of their own to work together as a team and improve performance.
Lesson 2	*Reflecting to Gain Perspectives* ❏ **Trade Book Focus:** *The True Story of the Three Little Pigs* by Jon Scieszka ❏ **Practice Activity:** "A Bit at a Time": Students will be shown a series of images, each one adding a single new detail. At each step, students will be asked if they think they know what the picture portrays, but they must be careful not to jump to conclusions!
Authentic Application Activity	*Choose Your Path Story* ❏ **Practice Activity:** Students will read the Choose Your Path story "Success at the Science Fair," making choices and reflecting on how those choices affect their eventual success. They will reflect on their path through the story with a reflection worksheet. As an extension, students will be invited to create their own Choose Your Path story.

DOI: 10.4324/9781003268307-6

Reflection Lesson 1: Reflecting on Experiences

Objective: Introduce the concept of reflection, defining the skill as thinking about what we know in order to improve outcomes.

Materials

- ❏ *Millie Fierce* by Jane K. Manning (teacher's copy)
- ❏ Handout 5.2: Read Aloud Reflection (one per student)
- ❏ Technology equipment to project a short video clip: "The Bridge"
  - ■ Video Link: https://youtu.be/_X_AfRk9F9w
- ❏ Flat, moveable objects to serve as "magic stones," such as round rubber spot markers, small carpet squares, construction paper, etc. (enough for each team to have one less "stone" than there are team members)
- ❏ Cones or tape to mark start and end lines in Skill Development Activity
- ❏ Stopwatches (one for each team) or a large timer (counting up) projected for the whole class to see
- ❏ Handout 5.3: Reflection Activity Recording Sheet (one per student)

Whole Group Introduction

- ❏ Introduce the next convergent thinking skill: **reflection**. Tell students that reflection means looking at our experiences, knowledge, and ideas, and taking the time to organize our thoughts before jumping to conclusions. Reflection is important because it leads to thinking carefully about the information we have in order to arrive at or improve solutions.
- ❏ Show the Reflection Anchor Chart and remind students that we need to take time and reflect before we finalize our thinking.

Read Aloud Activity

- ❏ Discuss the concept of reflecting on our own experiences in effort to do better next time. Ask students to think of a time when they've

Handout 5.1: Reflection Anchor Chart

REFLECTION

TAKING TIME TO THINK
CAREFULLY ABOUT THE FACTS

looked back on how an event happened for them (a test, a sports game, a speech, even an interaction with peers/adults/siblings), and wished they could have a re-do, or thought of something they could have done differently. Take a few minutes to share.

- ❑ Explain that today's book is about a girl who doesn't like the way things are going for her, so she decides to change them herself. Tell students to look for places where they see the main character **reflecting**, both on her experiences and feelings and on how others respond to her.
- ❑ Read aloud *Millie Fierce*.
- ❑ Discuss the book and how reflection plays a role using the Read Aloud Reflection page (Handout 5.2). Key understandings for this reflection are outlined in Box 5.1.

Box 5.1: *Millie Fierce* Key Understandings

- ❑ *Story summary*: Tired of not being noticed, Millie decides to become "fierce." She gains notice by doing naughty and unkind things. Slowly, she realizes that this is not a kind of attention that she wants to receive. She decides to return to being herself, and leaves being fierce in the past.
- ❑ *Connection to reflection*: Millie notices how her actions affect others. Reflecting on the consequences of her actions leads her to decide to stop being "Millie Fierce."
- ❑ *Sequence of events*: Millie's drawing gets destroyed, and no one notices. She decides to behave in ways that will get others' attention, and begins acting fiercely. She does things that are unkind and naughty. When her fierce behavior ruins a birthday party for a classmate, Millie feels guilty and decides that gaining attention for being fierce is not the best way to gain attention.
- ❑ *Cause and effect*: Millie turned fierce to get attention from people who had overlooked her. She returns to normal after seeing the effect her behavior has on others.
- ❑ *Consequences of being fierce*: Millie got the attention she wanted, but nobody wanted to be around her. They looked at her from afar, rather than interacting with her. She wasn't overlooked, but she also didn't gain any friends.
- ❑ *Implications*: A better way to get attention would be to carry out positive actions.

Handout 5.2: Read Aloud Reflection

Millie Fierce by Jane K. Manning

Name: ______________________________

Summarize the main idea of the story.	How did the characters use reflection in the story?

Give a brief summary of the events of the book. You can make a list, timeline, or write a few sentences.

What caused Millie to turn fierce? What caused her to return to (mostly) normal?

What were the consequences of Millie being fierce? Did she get what she wanted?

Reflect on this story: What is a better way to get attention than being fierce?

Skill Development Activity

- ❏ Remind students that as much as we can reflect on our own actions, we can also learn lessons by reflecting on the actions and experiences of others. Tell them they will see a short clip that illustrates this concept.
- ❏ Show students the animated short "Bridge."
  - ■ Video Link: https://youtu.be/_X_AfRk9F9w
  - ■ *Teacher's note*: Always preview content before showing to students. Ensure you have the correct video and that you are in ad-free mode.
- ❏ Discuss how characters watched others and worked together to find a good solution. How did **reflection** play a role here?
- ❏ Tell students that next they will play the "Lava Crossing" game, where they will have to cross an area of "lava" without touching the floor. If students touch the floor in any way, the whole team will have to go back to the start and begin again. Divide into teams of four to six.
- ❏ Pass out "magic stones," one fewer than the number of members in each team. These can be round rubber spot markers, pieces of construction paper, or even small carpet squares—use what you have available! You want the stones to be small (about the right size for two feet to be on them at a time), moveable, and flat. Students will be walking across these (imagining they are stepping-stones), so you want them to be something students can stand on without having to balance on an unsteady surface or having them slide from under their feet.
- ❏ Designate the lava crossing zone (an 8–10 foot stretch of floor). Mark the start and end lines with tape or cones.
- ❏ Tell students that their goal is to get their entire team across the lava zone, but they can only step on "magic stones." In an extra twist, any magic stone that is not in direct contact with a human will evaporate and be gone. Students cannot step on the lava (floor), or else the whole team must go back and start again. They want to make this crossing as quickly as possible.
- ❏ Have them work as teams to figure out how to cross the lava. Designate one team member to be the "timer" for each team, starting the stop-watch when the team begins and stopping it only once the whole team has safely crossed the lava. Note: If you want to use a large projected stopwatch, be sure that it is counting up (not down), and that you start it at a common signal time for all teams. If a projected stopwatch is used, each team's timer should simply make a note of the time on the screen when their team is finished.
- ❏ Watch as students complete the activity. As students cross:
  - ■ Pick up any stones left untouched by team members along the way.
  - ■ Provide encouragement to teams who seem stuck.

Handout 5.3: Reflection Activity Recording Sheet

Name: ______________________________

LAVA CROSSING

- **Your Goal:** Cross the floor without touching the lava!
- **Your Tools:** Magic Stones—these magical stones can be placed on the lava to help you cross but watch out; if they're not in constant contact with a human they lose their magic and burn up in the lava!
- **Don't Forget:** Your whole team needs to be able to cross safely! If one member touches the lava, you all must start again. Try to cross as quickly and safely as you can!

Crossing #1

What went well?

What was challenging?

How fast did your team cross?

Did you lose any Magic Stones along the way?

What could your team do to improve your performance for your next crossing?

Crossing #2

What went well?

What was challenging?

How fast did your team cross?

Did you lose any Magic Stones along the way?

How did reflection on your first crossing make this crossing better?

On the back, write instructions for this activity for a new group of students. Be sure to include what you learned through reflection so that they can be successful!

- Ensure timers are using their stopwatches correctly.
- Watch for students who touch the lava (stepping off of their team's magic stones). If this happens, send the whole team back to the start!

❑ Discuss team strategies: What worked? What didn't? Guide the teams in discussing amongst themselves how to improve their team's performance.

❑ Complete the activity again—how did reflection help us to improve our performance (Time? Efficiency? Easier to communicate/work together?).

❑ As a whole group, discuss the following: How did reflection help us in this activity? Could we have done as well without reflecting on our performance?

Reflection Lesson 2: Reflecting to Gain Perspectives

Objective: Develop the skill of withholding judgment until as many facts as possible have been gathered.

Materials

❑ Handout 5.4: The Three Little Pigs (teacher's copy)

❑ *The True Story of the Three Little Pigs* by Jon Scieszka (teacher's copy)

❑ Handout 5.5: Read Aloud Reflection Page

❑ Technology equipment to display short video: "Guess the Picture."
- https://youtu.be/Kffd0F1AYWU
- *Teacher's note*: The video comes from a YouTube channel with many different episodes of the "Guess the Picture" game. Feel free to choose any of the episodes; Episode 1 is linked here. Be sure to preview any episode before using it with students.

❑ Handout 5.6: "Guess the Picture" Recording Sheet

Whole Group Introduction

❑ Ask students to retell the familiar story of the Three Little Pigs. If students are not familiar with the traditional story, share a version of it with them, or read aloud the traditional English version included provided in Handout 5.4. *At this step, you will be focused on the **traditional** version of this story, not any alternate versions.* Ask:

Handout 5.4: Traditional Retelling of The Three Pigs

There was an old sow with three little pigs, and as she had not enough to keep them, she sent them out to seek their fortune. The first that went off met a man with a bundle of straw, and said to him, "Please, man, give me that straw to build me a house."

Which the man did, and the little pig built a house with it. Presently came along a wolf, and knocked at the door, and said, "Little pig, little pig, let me come in."

To which the pig answered, "No, not, by the hair of my chinny-chin-chin."

The wolf then answered to that, "Then I'll huff, and I'll puff, and I'll blow your house in." So he huffed, and he puffed, and he blew his house in, and ate up the little pig.

The second little pig met a man with a bundle of furze, and said, "Please, man, give me that furze to build a house."

Which the man did, and the pig built his house. Then along came the wolf, and said, "Little pig, little pig, let me come in."

"No, not, by the hair of my chinny-chin-chin."

"Then I'll puff, and I'll huff, and I'll blow your house in."

So he huffed, and he puffed, and he puffed, and he huffed, and at last he blew the house down, and he ate up the little pig.

The third little pig met a man with a load of bricks, and said, "Please, man, give me those bricks to build a house with."

So the man gave him the bricks, and he built his house with them. So the wolf came, as he did to the other little pigs, and said, "Little pig, little pig, let me come in."

"No, not, by the hair of my chinny-chin-chin."

"Then I'll huff, and I'll puff, and I'll blow your house in."

Well, he huffed, and he puffed, and he huffed, and he puffed, and he puffed and huffed; but he could *not* get the house down. When he found that he could not, with all his huffing and puffing, blow the house down, he said, "Little pig, I know where there is a nice field of turnips."

"Where?" said the little pig.

"Oh, in Mr. Smith's home-field, and if you will be ready tomorrow morning, I will call for you, and we will go together, and get some for dinner."

"Very well," said the little pig, "I will be ready. What time do you mean to go?"

"Oh, at six o'clock."

Handout 5.4, continued: Traditional Retelling of The Three Pigs

Well, the little pig got up at five, and got the turnips before the wolf came (which he did about six) and who said, "Little Pig, are you ready?"

The little pig said, "Ready! I have been and come back again and got a nice potful for dinner."

The wolf felt very angry at this but thought that he would trick the little pig somehow or other, so he said, "Little pig, I know where there is a nice apple-tree."

"Where?" said the pig.

"Down at Merry-garden," replied the wolf, "and if you will not deceive me, I will come for you, at five o'clock tomorrow and get some apples."

Well, the little pig bustled up the next morning at four o'clock, and went off for the apples, hoping to get back before the wolf came. But he had further to go, and had to climb the tree, so that just as he was coming down from it, he saw the wolf coming, which, as you may suppose, frightened him very much. When the wolf came up, he said, "Little pig, what! Are you here before me? Are they nice apples?"

"Yes, very," said the little pig. "I will throw you down one."

And he threw it so far, that, while the wolf was gone to pick it up, the little pig jumped down and ran home. The next day the wolf came again, and said to the little pig, "Little pig, there is a fair this afternoon, will you go?"

"Oh yes," said the pig, "I will go; what time shall you be ready?"

"At three," said the wolf. So the little pig went off before the time as usual, got to the fair, and bought a butter-churn, which he was going home with, when he saw the wolf coming. Then he could not tell what to do. So he got into the churn to hide, and by so doing, turned it round, and it rolled down the hill with the pig in it, which frightened the wolf so much, that he ran home without going to the fair.

He went to the little pig's house and told him how frightened he had been by a great round thing, which came down the hill past him. Then the little pig said, "Hah, I frightened you, then. I had been to the fair and bought a butter-churn, and when I saw you, I got into it, and rolled down the hill."

Then the wolf was very angry indeed, and declared he *would* eat up the little pig, and that he would get down the chimney after him. When the little pig saw what he was about, he hung on the pot full of water, and made up a blazing fire, and, just as the wolf was coming down, took off the cover, and in fell the wolf. So the little pig put on the cover again in an instant, boiled him up, ate him for supper, and lived happy ever afterwards.

- Who was/were the good guy(s)? How do you know?
- Who was/were the bad guy(s)? How do you know?
- Ask students to consider the following: are there any parts or perspectives in this story that are untold? What do we not know? What details does the story not tell us?

Read Aloud Activity

- ❑ Invite students to consider how the traditional story of the Three Little Pigs might be different if considered from another perspective. Ask them to reflect upon how the wolf, perhaps, might have felt about the pigs' tricks.
- ❑ Read aloud *The True Story of the Three Little Pigs* by Jon Scieszka. As you read, ask students to pause at various intervals and think about how this story is similar to/different from the original.
- ❑ After reading, ask:
  - Who was/were the good guy(s)? How do you know?
  - Who was/were the bad guy(s)? How do you know
  - Independently or with a partner, students should complete the Read Aloud Reflection page (Handout 5.5) to reflect on the story. See Box 5.2 for key understandings from this Read Aloud Reflection.
- ❑ Discuss the following: On further reflection, whose narrative of the story is more believable? What evidence do we have to support what is true about this story?

Box 5.2: *The True Story of the Three Little Pigs* Key Understandings

- ❑ *Story summary*: In this retelling of the classic tale of The Three Little Pigs, the Big Bad Wolf is painted as a sympathetic figure who only wanted to borrow a cup of sugar from the three pigs, but ends up destroying their houses when he huffs and puffs due to a seasonal cold.
- ❑ *Connection to reflection*: The wolf's reflection on the story is from an entirely new perspective. He feels like the victim, and thinks about how he could have done things differently so he might not have been cast as "bad."

Handout 5.5: Read Aloud Reflection

The True Story of the Three Little Pigs by Jon Scieszka

Name: ____________________

Summarize the main idea of the story.

How did the Wolf's reflection on the events match/differ from what you have heard about this story in the past?

Compare and contrast what you know of the traditional "Three Little Pigs" story to this story using the Venn diagram below.

Until the Wolf told his side of the story, most people have probably believed the traditional story of what happened to the Three Little Pigs. What does this story teach us about believing everything we hear?

- ❑ *Compare and contrast*: Students should recognize that while many key elements are the same (the number of pigs, the fact that the wolf blows down the pigs' houses), details about the order and intent of events differ based on the narrator.
- ❑ *Lessons from the story*: Students should recognize that each character's perspective affects how they feel about the events of the story. There are always two sides/perspectives to an event, and it is helpful to reflect on various perspectives when making judgments.

Skill Development Activity

- ❑ Tell students to think about how, when solving problems, it is important to have as complete a picture as possible, considering an expanding perspective before making a determination about a solution.
- ❑ Today, students will participate in a visual reflection activity that asks them to think about what they see in order to make a determination about a solution. In this activity, students will be presented with a bit of visual information at a time, and they will work to piece together what they have seen to figure out what the final picture will show. Distribute the "Guess the Picture" recording sheet (Handout 5.6).
- ❑ Display the video clip of the "Guess the Picture" game. In this clip, students will be shown a series of images, each zoomed in to very close magnitude and slowly zoomed out to reveal the larger picture.
  - ■ https://youtu.be/Kffd0F1AYWU
  - ■ The video clip consists of five separate images. Each image starts zoomed in very closely. Pause the video as each image first appears on the screen. Students should write down their first guess about what the image is. Then, un-pause and let the clip play. The image will zoom out until students can see the entire image. Pause once the whole image is revealed and ask students to record the actual image in the corresponding space on their handout. Repeat this process for each of the images in the video clip.
  - ■ Guide students through the reflection questions to help summarize the reflection process in this activity.
  - ■ Discuss the following with the students: What does it mean to jump to conclusions? How is it beneficial to wait until we have complete information before we determine a final solution? Encourage the key understanding that it is beneficial to examine things fully before arriving at solutions; otherwise, our solutions may be inaccurate or incomplete.

Handout 5.6: Guess the Picture Recording Sheet

Name: ____

Watch the video clips. There will be several images presented, each giving a little bit more information on each slide. Use your skills in reflection (thinking before you jump to a conclusion) to see if you can guess each image! Record your guess before the final image is shown, and then record what each final image really is in the table below.

Image 1	My guess is…	The image is really…
Image 2	My guess is…	The image is really…
Image 3	My guess is…	The image is really…
Image 4	My guess is…	The image is really…
Image 5	My guess is…	The image is really…

Which image was easiest to guess? What made it easy?

Which image was trickiest to guess? What made it tricky?

What does it mean to "jump to conclusions"?

What can be consequences of jumping to conclusions?

How does reflection help us avoid jumping to conclusions?

Reflection Authentic Application Activity: Choose Your Path Story

Objective: Practice the skill of reflection in an authentic context.

Materials

- ❑ Handout 5.7: Choose Your Path Mini-Booklet (one per student, prepared in advance; see directions in box 5.1)
- ❑ Handout 5.8: Choose Your Path Reflection

Whole Group Introduction

- ❑ Review with students the process of using **reflection**. Emphasize that in order to reflect, we must use information available to use in order to think back through decisions we have already made and make improvements.
- ❑ Provide the entry point of reflecting on a few examples together as a group:
  - ■ If you felt like you didn't need to study for a test, and instead went outside to play with friends after school, but later didn't do well on the test, how would you reflect on this choice?
  - ■ Your mom has a basil plant that she keeps on the windowsill in the kitchen. Lately, it's been looking pretty wilted and droopy. Thinking back, you can't remember the last time you saw your mom water it. Reflecting on what you know about plants and what you've seen, what could you do to help?
  - ■ Think about this last week of school. You're all working hard and learning, but as you reflect, is there something you could improve?
  - ■ What do you think is meant by the saying "hindsight is 20/20"?

Skill Development Activity

- ❑ Tell students that we often must make choices, only knowing later if what we've chosen will work out well for us. Today, they will be reading a story and making choices along the way.
- ❑ Prepare the "Success at the Science Fair" (Handout 5.7) story by folding mini-booklets for each student (see Box 5.3).

Convergent Thinking Skills:
Reflection

SUCCESS AT THE SCIENCE FAIR

a choose your path story

Handout 5.7: Choose Your Path Mini-Book

Your hard work, good choices, and scientific savvy have paid off. You won! Great job. The judges can't wait to see what great project you come up with next year!

When your teacher first mentioned the science fair, it sounded boring. But after you saw some of the awesome projects kids had done in the past, you started to change your mind. How cool would it be to build an actual exploding volcano? Or make a light bulb work with just a potato? Or even show how to suck an egg into a jar?

The next day, you go to the sign up board, ready to add your name to the list of kids entering the science fair. To your shock, there are already 12 kids signed up! This is some stiff competition. What will you do?

I'm too nervous. There's no way I can win with that kind of competition. Maybe I'll wait and do the science fair next year.

Turn to page 10.

Well, there's no time like the present. I'll have to work extra hard to make my science project stand out with this much competition! I'm in.

Turn to page 2.

Now that you've signed up for the fair, you have to come up with a project idea. This is a tough one—you really want to impress those judges!

You start to think of ideas, but none of them seem quite right. All you can think about is how great some of the old projects your teacher showed you were, and how much fun it would be to make a volcano explode!

After working on ideas without picking one for an hour, you're tired and frustrated. What do you do?

I'll take a break and think about it tomorrow. I need to come up with something original if I want to be competitive!

Turn to page 4.

If it was good enough to win last year, it's good enough for me. I'm making the volcano. I'm sure I'll find a way to put my own spin on it!

Turn to page 10.

You thought you knew what you were talking about, but when the judges questioned your scientific evidence, you couldn't think of what to say! It was obvious that you didn't do enough research to support your experiment.

Turn to page 10.

You've planned, researched, experimented, and prepared—now it's finally science fair day! You're all ready to go with your presentation and it's exciting to be there!

Looking around, you see several of your friends also displaying their projects. The judges haven't come to your booth yet, but they will in a little while. You'd love to go see some of your friends' projects, too. What will you do?

I need to stay at my booth and wait for the judges. I can't go anywhere.

Turn to page 7.

The judges could be a while—I can run over and see one or two friends while I wait and be back before they come to my project.

Turn to page 10.

Uh-oh. This did not go well. You're not proud of the way you presented, and you definitely didn't win a ribbon.

Thinking back on it, you know now where you went wrong. What could you have done differently?

Reflect on your choices and try again! Go back to page 1 to re-start your science fair journey.

After the movie, you stayed up late to work on your project, but ended up falling asleep before you were able to finish. You throw the last couple of things onto your board with only a few minutes to spare before the fair, and you know it's not your best work. Maybe the movie wasn't the best idea after all?

Turn to page 10.

You've finally finished your board, and it's looking GREAT. Next you need to put the finishing touches on your oral report. When you get to the science fair, the judges will come around and each participant will have to talk about their project. You're nervous about this part!

Your parents have offered to let you practice your report in front of them, but you're just not sure. What do you do?

It's super uncomfortable and makes you feel nervous, but you agree to practice in front of your parents and little brother a couple of times.

Turn to page 12.

Practicing in front of your parents is weird. They have to say they like it—they're your parents! You decide to read your notes over in bed the night before the fair. You'll be fine!

Turn to page 6.

Great job—you finally came up with a topic! You're going to test the acidity of some different drinks and see which ones are best for cleaning coins. Now you need to really dig in and do some research so that you can come up with a hypothesis and do your experiment.

Research is hard work, and you're really struggling to find facts that help you make a hypothesis. The internet is a big place, and it's hard to know what is a good fact and what is not! After spending an hour researching and with only a couple of good facts to show for it, you're tired. What do you do?

I've had all of these drinks before and I know which ones are sour. I'll just use that—it's plenty of information.

Turn to page 11.

I'll ask the school librarian for help tomorrow. He always knows where to look for good information!

Turn to page 5.

It's a good thing you took the full three days to re-do your experiment. Now you have great, accurate scientific data to use to make a claim about your hypothesis!

With all that data, you have a lot to do to create your presentation board. You need to make charts and graphs, write the results in a paragraph, and attach pictures of your experiment to the board. Just as you get started, your best friend calls and invites you to see the newest movie at the theater with them. You really want to go, but if you do, you will have less time to finish your presentation board for the fair. What do you do?

I wish I could see the movie with my friend, but I need to finish this project. It's not as much fun, but I have a lot to do and want to make sure I can complete it.

Turn to page 9.

I already have all the information I need—how long could it take to attach it to the board? I have time for a movie. I'll finish the project later.

Turn to page 3.

You're finally getting somewhere, and you feel great about the way your project is going. You're testing your hypothesis with pennies in cola, lemonade, milk, and water. You had planned to leave the coins in the drinks for three days, but you put them in on Thursday afternoon and now you're going to the beach with your family for the weekend.

You're faced with a choice: what do you do?

I'll go ahead and take out the coins on Friday afternoon and report on that. I know it doesn't match my hypothesis **exactly**, but I'm sure it's close enough.

Turn to page 11.

I'm going to take the coins out today and re-start my experiment next week when I can take the three days I had planned to in my hypothesis.

Turn to page 10.

Thank goodness you didn't go anywhere—here come the judges! They're smiling, and they seem to love your project. You nailed your speech and your extra time in the library helped you answer all of their extra questions. You feel great about how you did at the fair!

Turn to page 13.

You had it down so well in your head, but when it came time to actually do your presentation out loud for the judges, you got nervous and stumbled over your words. You're pretty sure you left out a whole section of your project! You wish you had practiced the speech for a real audience before the fair.

Turn to page 10.

Box 5.3: Mini-Booklet Assembly Instructions: How to Prepare Mini-Booklets

1. Fold the first page in half, ensuring that the fold is at the bottom and the front cover is on top (facing you).
2. Fold the first page in half again so that the creases are on the left and bottom and the cover is still facing you.
3. Repeat the same folds for each of the other pages, ensuring that the creases are on the bottom and left sides and that the odd-numbered pages are on top.
4. Insert each of the folded interior pages inside the front cover page, ensuring that the pages are numbered sequentially. Close the book and adjust the pages to square up the edges.
5. Staple the booklet twice along the folded edge of the front cover to hold the interior pages in place. If desired, place a strip of tape along the stapled edge to cover the staples, trimming any excess.

- ❑ Ask students, either independently or with a partner, to read through the story, making choices where indicated. Encourage them to reflect on choices and try again until they are successful in reaching the end of the story and winning the science fair.
- ❑ Distribute the reflection page (Handout 5.8) and ask students to thoughtfully reflect on how they made choices throughout the story.
- ❑ Discuss answers to reflection questions as a class.
- ❑ Summarize the activity with the emphasis that we must reflect on choices in order to learn and grow. We can be more effective problem-solvers when we use reflection on past choices to help us improve our futures!
- ❑ Ask students to reflect on the structure of the Choose Your Path story. See if they can create a map of where each choice led.
- ❑ Extension: Encourage students to create their own stories using the template created by analyzing this story. Their story should begin with a new scenario of their choosing. They can publish this story in book format, or they may use PowerPoint/Google Slides (linking choices to corresponding slides) or other technology to present their stories if desired. Note that this writing activity is highly complex. Some ways to scaffold supports for students are the following:
  - ■ Allow students to work with a partner to develop their story.

Handout 5.8: Choose Your Path Reflection

Name: ____

You had to make a lot of tough decisions in order to be successful at the science fair. Each choice impacted the success (or failure!) of your project in some way. Reflect on how you were able to be successful.

Answer the questions below. Be prepared to share!

What was the hardest decision you had to make? Why?

Did any decisions seem obvious, even before you made them? Explain.

What decisions helped you to succeed? Explain.

Which decisions would have caused you to lose the fair? Explain.

Reflect on a time you did a project in real life. What similarities do you see between your own project and the story?

What advice would you give someone who is starting a big project, like a science fair presentation, after completing this activity?

    - ■ Encourage students to begin with a familiar story context, such as that of a well-known fairy or folk tale.
    - ■ Allow students to use the existing model story, "Success at the Science Fair," but alter the possible choices or scenario specifics.
- ❏ If time allows, encourage students to share their stories with others and/or display their stories for others to enjoy.

Reflection Concluding Activities

- ❏ Distribute the Reflection Exit Ticket (Appendix A). Ask students to reflect on their learning about the skill using reflection to modify solution paths and gain perspective. Allow time for students to complete the exit ticket. Use this as a formative assessment, to gain a better understanding of your students' readiness to effectively practice the skill.
- ❏ If desired, complete the Group Reflection Rubric (Appendix A) to track students' progress with the skill.
- ❏ If desired, use the Convergent Thinking Student Observation Rubric (Appendix A) to assess and quantify individual students' mastery.
- ❏ Ask students to retrieve their Convergent Thinking Avatar (Handout I.3). In the Reflection box, they should either record the main ideas about the thinking skill or illustrate their avatar using the skill of reflection.

Bibliography

Guess the Picture. (April 22, 2020). Guess the Picture, Ep. 1. https://www.youtube.com/watch?v=KffdOF1AYWU.

Manning, J.K. (2012). *Millie Fierce.* New York: Philomel Books.

Scieszka, J. (1996). *The true story of the three little pigs.* New York: Puffin Books.

The Story of the Three Little Pigs. (n.d.). https://www.gutenberg.org/files/18155/18155-h/18155-h.htm.

Tey, T.C. (August 26, 2013). Bridge. https://www.youtube.com/watch?v=_X_AfRk9F9w.

Appendix A

Assessments

Several assessment options are provided in this unit. It is not necessary to use all of the provided options; rather, you should choose the options that work best for your own classroom needs.

One aspect to pay close attention to is the indicators associated with each thinking skill. These indicators provide an outline of expected behavioral outcomes for students. As you work through the lessons, keep an eye out for students who are able to achieve the indicators efficiently and effectively, as well as those who may need more support. The intent of this unit is to foster a mastery mindset; make note of student growth and skill development as you progress, rather than focusing on summative outcomes against specific benchmarks.

1. **Exit Tickets:** Exit tickets are provided to correspond with each sub-skill. These are intended to be formative, giving you a sense of students' mastery and self-efficacy with each skill. These tickets will also give you great insight into areas where a re-visit is warranted. If a student would benefit from additional instruction in a sub-skill area, consider using one or more of the extension options listed in Appendix B.
2. **Individual Student Observations:** This form is intended for use for each student individually. All five thinking skills are outlined on the page, and you can track individual student progress toward indicator goals easily. Use this form to gather data, report data to stakeholders, or simply help students see their own progress.

3. **Convergent Thinking Sub-Skill Group Observation Checklists:** This checklist is provided for each thinking skill. This is a great running measure of students' mastery of the indicators associated with each thinking skill. Each skill has three indicators for mastery, and you can track student progress toward these goals as a group using this form.
4. **Socratic Seminar Assessment**: Provided here is a rubric for assessment after completion of Socratic Seminar. Also included is a form for students to self-evaluate their performance in this unique learning experience.

Handout A.1: Observation Exit Ticket

Name: ______________________________

Date: ______________________________

Observation is...

The easiest part about observation is...

The trickiest part about observation is...

How confident I feel about observation:

Your opinion (feelings, questions, ideas, favorite parts) of this unit:

Handout A.2: Evidence Exit Ticket

Name: ______________________________

Date: ______________________________

Using evidence is…

The easiest part about using evidence is…

The trickiest part about using evidence is…

How confident I feel about using evidence :

Your opinion (feelings, questions, ideas, favorite parts) of this unit:

Handout A.3: Inferencing Exit Ticket

Name: ______________________________

Date: ______________________________

Inferencing is…

The easiest part about inferencing is…

The trickiest part about inferencing is…

How confident I feel about inferencing:

Your opinion (feelings, questions, ideas, favorite parts) of this unit:

Handout A.4: Deduction Exit Ticket

Name: ______________________________
Date: ______________________________

Deduction is...

The easiest part about deduction is...

The trickiest part about deduction is...

How confident I feel about deduction:

Your opinion (feelings, questions, ideas, favorite parts) of this unit:

Handout A.5: Reflection Exit Ticket

Name: ______________________________

Date: ______________________________

Reflection is…

The easiest part about reflection is…

The trickiest part about reflection is…

How confident I feel about reflection:

Your opinion (feelings, questions, ideas, favorite parts) of this unit:

Handout A.6: Individual Student Observation Rubric

Student name:

Masterful	Exceeds expectations
Proficient	Independent mastery
Developing	Success with scaffolding
Beginning	Not yet achieved

	MASTERFUL (4)	PROFICIENT (3)	DEVELOPING (2)	BEGINNING (1)
OBSERVATION • Make use of all five senses • Note and fully describe both large and small details • Consider perspectives of others				
	Notes:			
USING EVIDENCE • Finds factual evidence in text to support claims • Cites evidence in supporting arguments • Bases claims in facts and observations				
	Notes:			
INFERENCING • Bases thinking off of observable evidence • Identified missing components/info • Combines knowns with unknows to infer				
	Notes;			
DEDUCTION • Uses clues to eliminate possibilities • Draws logical conclusions • Uses clues to confirm possibilities				
	Notes:			
REFLECTION • Revisit problems to develop alternate solution paths • Avoid hasty conclusions • Analyze solutions from various perspectives				
	Notes:			

Handout A.7: Observation Group Checklist

*	Exceeds expectations
+	Independent mastery
✓	Success with scaffolding
o	Not yet achieved

Students	Indicators		
	Make use of all five senses	Note and fully describe details, both large and small	Consider the perspectives of others

Handout A.8: Using Evidence Group Checklist

*	Exceeds expectations
+	Independent mastery
✓	Success with scaffolding
o	Not yet achieved

Students	Indicators		
	Find factual evidence from text to support given claims	Cite evidence in supporting arguments	Base claims on facts and observations

Handout A.9: Inferencing Group Checklist

*	Exceeds expectations
+	Independent mastery
✓	Success with scaffolding
o	Not yet achieved

Students	**Indicators**		
	Base thinking off of observable evidence	Identify missing components/ information	Combine knowns with unknowns to infer

Handout A.10: Deduction Group Checklist

*	Exceeds expectations
+	Independent mastery
✓	Success with scaffolding
o	Not yet achieved

Students	**Indicators**		
	Use clues to eliminate possibilites	Use clues to confirm possibilities	Draw logical conclusions

Handout A.11: Reflection Group Checklist

*	Exceeds expectations
+	Independent mastery
✓	Success with scaffolding
o	Not yet achieved

Students	Indicators		
	Revisit problems to develop alternate solution paths	Avoid making hasty conclusions	Analyze solutions from various perspectives

Handout A.12: Socratic Seminar Self-Reflection

Name: ______________________________

Date: ______________________________

Something I did well is:

Something I wish I had done differently is:

This part of my thinking stayed the same:

This part of my thinking changed:

How I feel Socratic Seminar went for our group today:

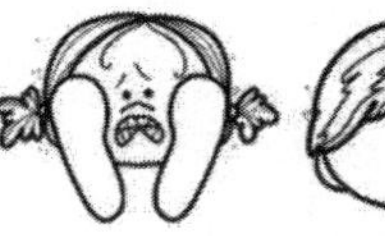   

Your opinion (feelings, questions, ideas, favorite parts) of this Socratic Seminar:

Handout A.13: Socratic Seminar Rubric

	Exemplary	Proficient	Developing	Beginning
Preparation	Student has read the text multiple times, taken notes, highlights key words or phrases.	Student has read the material and has a good understanding.	Student appears to have skimmed the article, but shows little reflection prior to the seminar.	Student is unprepared. Has not read the article or taken notes.
Content Knowledge	Student skillfully analyzes and interprets the information. Student provides meaningful references to the text.	Student compiles and interprets the information effectively. Student provides some references to the text.	Student compiles and lists facts from the text.. Student relies heavily on opinions but is unable to support with text.	Student requires teacher guidance to compile ideas. Requires frequent prompting.
Reasoning	Student cites relevant text evidence. Makes connections to other topics. Asks questions to further the dialogue. Willing to hear/take on other viewpoints.	Student cites some text evidence. Makes limited connections to others' ideas. May be able to hear other viewpoints.	Misses main points of the dialogue. May have some misunderstandings. Limited textual support. Refuses to acknowledge other viewpoints.	Comments do not make sense with the dialogue. Can't stay with the conversation..
Communicates thinking and reasoning effectively	Student is able to discuss thinking clearly, supporting claims with evidence and responding to claims of others. Builds on the ideas of others.	Student is able to discuss thinking clearly and support their own claims. May build on the ideas of others.	Student is able to discuss their own thinking clearly. Limited connecting or building upon the ideas of others.	Student participates in discussion, and is able to communicate effectively with teacher guidance.
Listening	Pays attention to details. Listens to others respectfully by making eye contact with the speaker and waiting their turn to speak. Asks for clarification.	Generally pays attention to others. Listens to others by making some eye contact with the speaker. May be too absorbed in their own ideas to actively engage in the discussion.	Appears to listen on and off throughout the seminar. May find some ideas unimportant and/or may be confused and not ask for clarification.	Student is uninvolved in the Socratic Seminar. Lots of misunderstanding due to inattention.
Conduct	Student demonstrates respect for others and follows the discussion. Participates but does not control the conversation.	Generally demonstrates respect for others and follows the discussion. May show some impatience with other view points. Avoids controlling the conversation.	Participates but tends to debate more than offer dialogue or is too timid to add to the conversation. May try to win. May engage in sidebar conversations.	Displays little respect for the learning process and interrupts frequently. Comments are not related or inappropriate.

Notes:

Appendix B

Extensions

Alternate Trade Books

In some cases, not all the trade books referenced within this unit may be readily available, or they may not be suited for your classroom environment, preferences, or audience. In other cases, you may choose to expand or deepen student understanding through an additional example rooted in rich text. Books listed in Table B.1 are suggestions for further study or to take the place of any of the read-aloud trade books suggested throughout the unit. Also included is a blackline master Read Aloud Reflection (Handout B.1), which can be used with any book of your choice to target the specified thinking skill.

TABLE B.1
Suggested Alternate Trade Books

Convergent Thinking Sub-Skill	Suggested Alternate Trade Books/Guiding Questions
Observation	❑ *Enigma* by Graeme Base ■ Can you find all the lost objects and observe the secret code? ❑ *Animalia* by Graeme Base ■ Can you observe all the ways that each letter of the alphabet is used? ❑ *The Lost House* by B.B. Cronin ■ How does color affect our ability to easily observe? ❑ *Anansi and the Moss-Covered Rock* by Eric A. Kimmel ■ Who is using observation keenly to trick the trickster?
Using Evidence	❑ *Grumpy Monkey* by Suzanne Lang ■ Jim insists that he's not grumpy—sadly, all evidence points to the fact that he is! ❑ *The Eleventh Hour* by Graeme Base ■ This book is a great wrap-up, where evidence found in every illustration puzzles the reader. ❑ *Mystery Mansion* by Michael Garland ■ A young boy finds a series of notes that are clues to a puzzle from his aunt.
Inferencing	❑ *Who Done It?* by Olivier Tallec ■ Very similar in style and structure to *Who What Where*? and with the same focus. ❑ *I Want My Hat Back* and/or *We Found a Hat* by Jon Klassen ■ Very similar in style to *This Is Not My Hat*, but with an added need to observe each illustration closely. ❑ *A Hungry Lion, or a Dwindling Assortment of Animals* by Lucy Ruth Cummins ■ Where do all of Lion's friends keep disappearing to? The answer may not be what you think! ❑ *Ring! Yo?* by Chris Raschka ■ Can you infer what is happening on the other side of the phone call?

Convergent Thinking Sub-Skill	Suggested Alternate Trade Books/Guiding Questions
Deduction	❏ *Detective LaRue* by Mark Teague ■ Follow LaRue as he deduces where the cats have gone and why. ❏ *The Mystery of the Missing Cake* by Claudia Boldt ■ Help Fox as he tries to discover who took the missing piece of birthday cake. ❏ *The Eleventh Hour* by Graeme Base ■ Who stole Horace's feast? The clues are in the illustrations—this one can get very involved, but it's fun! ❏ *Who Done it?* by Olivier Tallec ■ Use visual clues to confirm/eliminate suspects and solve each page's riddle.
Reflection	❏ *Big Wolf and Little Wolf* by Nadine Brun-Cosme ■ How does Big Wolf's opinion of Little Wolf change after reflection? ❏ *The Bad Seed* by Pete Oswald ■ Examine how reflection on others' comments leads the "bad seed" to change behaviors. ❏ *Ira Sleeps Over* by Bernard Waber ■ How did Ira use others' ideas to make his choice? On reflection, what should he have done?

Handout B.1: Universal Read Aloud Reflection

Book Title:

Name: ______________________________

Summarize the main idea of the story.	How did the book connect to the focus skill?

What details from the text showcase the focus skill?

What patterns do you notice in your list from the question above?

What generalization (big idea) can you make about the focus skill based on this book?

Novel Study Extensions

Novels are a great way to extend learning about thinking skills, applying convergent thinking in a broader context. The novels listed below support the thinking skills of this unit. The novel study units will allow the students to apply the thinking skills while reading excellent literature.

- ❑ *The Westing Game* by Ellen Raskin
  - ■ In this classic whodunit, 16 heirs apparent are tasked with solving the mystery surrounding the demise of Mr. Sam Westing. Readers must be savvy in their observations, evidence collecting, and deduction to solve this fun and fast-paced mystery!
- ❑ *Chasing Vermeer* by Blue Balliett
  - ■ In this novel, two friends work against the clock to solve the mystery of a stolen painting by Renaissance master Johannes Vermeer! Puzzles abound, and the illustrations provide another opportunity for convergent thinkers to use observation and inference.
- ❑ *Book Scavenger* by Jennifer Bertman
  - ■ This fun mystery centers around two friends who are racing against time to follow clues they have found in a mysterious book. For an added challenge, students can also play along in the real-life Book Scavenger Hunt!
- ❑ *The London Eye Mystery* by Siobhan Dowd
  - ■ This missing-person mystery is told from the point of view of a young boy who is not neurotypical. His observations of the people and events that unfold will keep readers guessing until the very end.
- ❑ *The Puzzling World of Winston Breen* by Eric Berlin
  - ■ This is a wild mystery that combines a search for an ancient treasure buried beneath a mountain of clues hidden in puzzle form.
- ❑ *From the Mixed-Up Files of Mrs. Basil E. Frankweiler* by E.L. Konigsburg
  - ■ This classic novel centers around two siblings who steal away to live in the Metropolitan Museum of Art. While there, they find themselves fascinated by the disappearance of a mysterious statue and must use their powers of observation and search for evidence to solve the mystery.
- ❑ *The Parker Inheritance* by Varian Johnson
  - ■ This contemporary novel and Coretta Scott King Award Honor Book follows two friends, Candice and Brandon, who find a letter in their attic that threatens to uncover the mystery of why Candice's grandmother left their town in shame in the era of Jim Crow. Also in the letter are hints that whoever can solve the decades-old

mystery will be awarded with a fortune. The friends must use deduction, evidence, and bravery to solve the mystery.

- ❑ *The House of Dies Drear* by Virginia Hamilton
  - ■ In this classic novel, a family tries to unravel the mysteries surrounding their new home, which they find was once a stop on the Underground Railroad. This book explores the concept of perception and how prejudices can cloud our judgment.

Games to Enhance Convergent Thinking Skills

Many mass-market games can be used to hone convergent thinking skills. Some suggested games which target convergent thinking are listed here.

- ❑ **Clue** is a great classic convergent thinking game. Players must use the clues in their own hands, observing those which other players target, and employ deductive reasoning to determine a final solution. This game develops the skills of *using evidence, inferring, observation,* and *deduction* in game play.
- ❑ **Mastermind** is a code-breaking game for two players. Player one becomes the code maker and player two is the code breaker. The code breaker tries to guess the pattern while the maker provides feedback for each guess. This game requires *using evidence, deduction, observation,* and *reflection* to achieve a win!
- ❑ **Headbanz** is a game in which one player tries to guess a word placed on their forehead by asking questions of the group, who can see the word. This game requires *inferencing, finding evidence,* and *deduction.*
- ❑ **Outfoxed** is a dice rolling game in which players move around the board to find *evidence* and must use *deduction* to figure out whodunit!
- ❑ **Guess Who** requires players to ask questions based on *observations* to gather *evidence* about the card their opponent holds. Each question allows them to use *deduction* in eliminating some options, eventually landing at a guess about who their opponent is!
- ❑ **Battleship** is another classic game which uses some visual *evidence* along with spatial *deduction* to guess where each player's opponents' ships are located. Through careful *reflection,* players will be able to sink their partner's ships before they have to admit, "You sunk my battleship!"

Made in the USA
Monee, IL
07 November 2023